"This book is a brilliant synthesis of old and new. The authors have updated the powerful, life-affirming philosophy of Stoicism for a modern-day audience, keeping its ancient roots while infusing it with insights from contemporary approaches such as acceptance and commitment therapy (ACT). It's an excellent and easy-to-use workbook, that among other benefits, will help you to live by your values, unhook yourself from difficult thoughts, make room for difficult emotions, be compassionate to yourself, use your core values as a compass to guide you, and live mindfully. Highly recommended!"

—**Russ Harris**, physician, therapist, and author of *ACT Made Simple* and *The Happiness Trap*

"A really useful workbook, combining ancient wisdom and modern psychology to enable you to become wiser and more resilient. Successfully synthesizes Stoicism and Socrates with third-wave cognitive behavioral therapy (CBT) approaches like ACT and dialectical behavior therapy (DBT). A book I will be recommending to my therapy clients and therapist colleagues."

—**Tim LeBon**, author of *365 Ways to Be More Stoic*, accredited CBT therapist working in the NHS and private practice, and director of research for Modern Stoicism and the Aurelius Foundation

"Thousands of years before psychotherapy existed, the practical wisdom of Stoic philosophy changed lives and shaped global civilizations! Written by internationally renowned experts in Socratic thought and evidence-based psychotherapy, this book harnesses the power of Stoic wisdom and the best that psychological science has to offer. This is a method that helps you to feel deeply and live wisely. I loved it. Highly, highly recommended!"

—**Dennis Tirch, PhD**, director at The Center for Compassion Focused Therapy

"*The Stoicism Workbook* by Waltman, Codd, and Pierce is an excellent introduction to how we can use the classic ideas of the Greek and Roman Stoics to build resilience, acceptance, and wisdom. Highly readable and practical, the exercises and insights in this 'smart book' will help every reader cope better with their unrealistic expectations and unhelpful responses to the inevitable frustrations of daily life. The authors are to be commended for this important contribution. Highly recommended."

—**Robert L. Leahy, PhD**, author or editor of twenty-nine books, including *If Only...: Finding Freedom from Regret*, *The Worry Cure*, and *The Jealousy Cure*

"This book is a scholarly, engaging, and informative journey into the philosophical origins of CBT, namely Stoicism revisited. The Stoic skills reviewed provide guidance on how to conduct modern-day psychotherapy, and ways to bolster resilience in patients. This is a journey worth taking."

> —**Donald Meichenbaum, PhD**, research director of the Melissa Institute for
> Violence Prevention in Miami, FL

"This book provides a perfect guide for navigating life's inevitable challenges. The highly esteemed authors have successfully combined the wisdom of Stoicism with that of Socrates to present a perfect model of stability and consistency in times of crisis. If you want to embrace uncertainty and improve your resilience in times of global or personal crisis, you need to read and practice this book."

> —**Mehmet Sungur**, professor of psychiatry at Istanbul Kent University in Istanbul,
> Beck Institute International Advisory Committee member, and World Confederation
> of Behavioural and Cognitive Therapies executive board member

"Scott Waltman, R. Trent Codd III, and Kasey Pierce created a friendly, welcoming, and reflective workbook from their extensive insight and knowledge of Stoic philosophy. *The Stoicism Workbook* illuminates the quote from Nöel Coward, 'Work is more fun than fun.' The powerful exercises will guide you through the radiant wisdom of the Stoics. They feel like they are with you as wise guides on every page. *The Stoicism Workbook* encourages a deeper understanding of Stoicism, and can effect profound change in your life."

> —**Karen Duffy**, *New York Times* bestselling author of *Wise Up*, *Backbone*, and *Model Patient*;
> pain patient advocate and certified Hospice Chaplain; and board member of Stoicares,
> an organization that promotes Stoicism as a philosophy of care and well-being

"*The Stoicism Workbook* is a masterpiece of self-help. The authors manage to introduce Stoicism and cognitive flexibility by leading the reader on a journey of self-knowledge and self-awareness. In the end, don't be surprised if you really have managed to embrace Stoicism as a way of thinking and living. I highly recommend that you enjoy the ride."

> —**Carmem Beatriz Neufeld, PhD**, associate professor at the University of São Paulo,
> head of the Cognitive Behavioral Intervention and Research Laboratory, and president
> of the Latin American Federation of Cognitive and Behavioral Psychotherapies

THE
STOICISM
WORKBOOK

How the Wisdom of Socrates Can Help You Build Resilience & Overcome Anything Life Throws at You

SCOTT WALTMAN, PSYD
R. TRENT CODD III, EDS
KASEY PIERCE

New Harbinger Publications, Inc.

Publisher's Note

This publication is designed to provide accurate and authoritative information in regard to the subject matter covered. It is sold with the understanding that the publisher is not engaged in rendering psychological, financial, legal, or other professional services. If expert assistance or counseling is needed, the services of a competent professional should be sought.

NEW HARBINGER PUBLICATIONS is a registered trademark of New Harbinger Publications, Inc.

New Harbinger Publications is an employee-owned company.

Cover design by Sara Christian

Acquired by Ryan Buresh

Edited by Karen Levy

Printed in the United States of America

26   25   24

10   9   8   7   6   5   4   3   2   1   First Printing

Dedicated to all those who believed philosophy was out of their grasp but sought solace during times of adversity. This book is for you…as is ancient wisdom.

And for Hector.

Contents

Foreword vii

Introduction 1

Chapter 1 Stoicism and Emotional Resilience 3

Chapter 2 The Paradox of Control and Stoic Practices to Embrace Not Having It 17

Chapter 3 Virtues and Values Clarification 31

Chapter 4 How to Live like a Stoic 55

Chapter 5 From Demandingness to Acceptance 69

Chapter 6 Tolerating Discomfort and Decreasing Suffering 83

Chapter 7 From Criticism to Compassion: Non-Judgmentalness 103

Chapter 8 Stoic Interpersonal Skills 115

Chapter 9 Learning to Think like Socrates: Overcoming Double Ignorance 135

Chapter 10 A Self-Socratic Method: Using Socratic Thinking to Get Unstuck 147

References 179

Foreword

Less than twenty years ago, Stoicism was little more than an obscure niche subject in academic philosophy. Although millions of people owned books by famous Stoics such as Marcus Aurelius and Seneca, nobody thought of Stoicism as a *movement* within the modern self-improvement field. That changed quite rapidly, as the emergence of social media allowed people all over the world who had read the Stoics to form online communities. In 2008, William B. Irvine published *A Guide to the Good Life: The Ancient Art of Stoic Joy*, the first best-selling modern book on Stoicism. A few years later, Ryan Holiday's *The Obstacle Is the Way: The Timeless Art of Turning Trials into Triumph*, became a huge international bestseller, which confirmed Stoicism as a genre of modern self-help. Now it's difficult to keep track of the new books and articles being published on Stoicism every year.

The foundations of this Stoic renaissance were laid much earlier, though, in the 1950s, by Albert Ellis, one of the leading pioneers of cognitive behavioral therapy (CBT). Ellis, having become thoroughly disillusioned with the psychoanalytic therapy in which he had trained, decided to start again from scratch. He began developing what, at that time, he called simply "rational therapy" but later became known as rational-emotive behavior therapy (REBT). Ellis had read widely in the field of psychotherapy but also in related subjects, particularly philosophy. He recalled having first encountered the writings of Marcus Aurelius and Epictetus as a young man. As he began looking for an alternative to the psychoanalytic tradition, they suddenly appeared more relevant to him than ever before. Ellis was happy to credit the Stoics with anticipating his key ideas: "Many of the principles incorporated in the theory of rational-emotive psychotherapy are not new; some of them, in fact, were originally stated several thousand years ago, especially by the Greek and Roman Stoic philosophers," and he names Epictetus and Marcus Aurelius in particular as his influences in this regard (Ellis 1962, 35). (Ellis appears to have been less interested in Seneca, the other famous Stoic whose works survive today.)

Indeed, Stoicism became one of the main philosophical inspirations for the new approach to psychotherapy that Ellis was developing. When Aaron T. Beck published his seminal *Cognitive*

Therapy and the Emotional Disorders, he likewise said that "the philosophical underpinnings [of cognitive therapy] go back thousands of years, certainly to the time of the Stoics, who considered man's conceptions (or misconceptions) of events rather than the events themselves as the key to his emotional upsets" (Beck 1976, 3). In particular, the famous quote from Epictetus used by both Ellis and Beck to explain the role of cognition in their theory of emotion, and psychopathology, became almost a cliché among therapists: "People are disturbed not by events, but by their opinions about events." This quote is found in countless subsequent books on CBT. It is, however, the *only* reference to Stoicism mentioned by most of them. That subsequent neglect of Stoicism is surprising for several reasons:

1. Ellis, the original pioneer of cognitive behavioral therapy, refers to Stoicism many times throughout his writings, drawing on different passages from Epictetus and Marcus Aurelius, and he employs many other concepts and practices that appear indebted to Stoicism.

2. As Stoicism and CBT share virtually the same *premise* about the role of cognition in emotional problems, they're likely to arrive at similar *conclusions* about the best solutions, and we should therefore expect that Stoic contemplative practices might be worth investigating in order to gain new ideas for therapy strategies and techniques.

3. As Stoicism is not merely a therapy but a whole philosophy of life, it potentially offers a framework for developing CBT into a lifelong practice for self-improvement and developing general emotional resilience.

4. Many individuals who are not attracted to conventional self-help or therapy literature are nevertheless drawn to Stoicism, and it may therefore provide their only exposure to beneficial psychological advice similar to that found in CBT. For instance, Stoicism is popular with prison inmates and military personnel, who sometimes (mistakenly) view using self-help or psychotherapy as a sign of weakness and therefore to be avoided.

5. With the development of a "third wave" in CBT, consisting of mindfulness and acceptance-based approaches, emphasis has shifted to strategies such as developing cognitive mindfulness and clarifying personal values, which bear a striking resemblance to prominent aspects of ancient Stoicism.

The Stoicism Workbook is written by two experienced CBT clinicians and one layperson who has been applying Stoicism to everyday problems of living. I hope that it will help its readers discover the many ways in which Stoic philosophy and cognitive psychotherapy might complement each other. In particular, by incorporating recent "third wave" ideas from CBT, the authors help expand the range of comparisons between Stoicism and modern psychotherapy. Moreover, by drawing attention to the value of Stoicism and Socratic questioning for building *emotional resilience*, they help bridge the divide between clinical practice and general self-improvement, making the combination of Stoicism and CBT relevant and applicable to a much wider audience.

—Donald J. Robertson
Author of *How to Think Like a Roman Emperor:*
The Stoic Philosophy of Marcus Aurelius

Introduction

Do external matters that are out of your control distract you?
Allocate some time to acquire fresh and beneficial knowledge,
and put an end to being constantly tossed about.

—Marcus Aurelius, *Meditations* 7.2

During Marcus Aurelius's reign as emperor, in the year 165 CE, a devastating epidemic known as the Antonine plague swept through the Roman Empire. There are some accounts that suggest that the death count reached up to five million across the empire. Just as our modern-day pandemic caused societal disruptions, this ancient tumultuous shroud over Rome led to economic uncertainty, political instability, and social unrest. Marcus was a student of Stoic philosophy, and thus was able to maintain his equanimity by focusing on what he could control versus what he couldn't. He persevered, leading a nation as well as his nearly thirty legions by drawing upon his cultivated wisdom, courage, and, ultimately, inner resilience. He'd witnessed the deaths of some of his own children during this time, as well as his wife Faustina. Despite these losses, he saw his duties as emperor through, shouldering the burden of leadership and providing stability in a time of crisis. The mass loss was out of his control, but what he could do for the greater good of Rome was not.

Today, we're not only recovering from the loss of lives and jobs, and torn by political polarization, but also struggling to carry on with life's everyday challenges amid the disarray. As functioning members of communities, families, relationships, teams, and so on, we're expected each day to provide stability in times of crises. But what of our inner stability? Will it hold steady that we may bear the courage to face adversity head-on? Can we possibly flourish and thrive amid the chaos that surrounds us and the everyday troubles we all face? The answer is *yes*.

This workbook was written to act as a guide to help you navigate these challenges. It will provide tools to help you foster a Stoic mindset, which will give you the psychological flexibility to absorb an unexpected blow with wisdom and even grow as a result. This is resilience. To the mother who fights succumbing to despair after losing her job to the pandemic, to the newly divorced father who faces a future filled with uncertainty, to the student in need of clarity to see their setbacks as opportunities, and to the terminally ill in need of courage to face their fate with peace in their heart…*this book is for you and all those in need of Stoic resilience.*

CHAPTER 1

Stoicism and Emotional Resilience

Choose not to be harmed—and you won't be.
Don't feel affected—and you won't feel affected.

—Marcus Aurelius, *Meditations* 4.7

Stoicism is an ancient philosophy that focuses on flourishing in the face of adversity. This is possible through the adoption of the perspective (and cornerstone quote of the philosophy): "What troubles us are not the events themselves, but rather our own judgments about them" (Epictetus, *Enchiridion* 5). This means that if we allow ourselves to challenge our initial anger, sadness, or frustration, we can cultivate a more rational response to unfavorable circumstances, preserving our peace and enabling us to carry on. The goal of a Stoic life isn't to avoid emotions or discomfort but rather to find strength and steadiness by focusing on what's within the realm of our control. A Stoic life is characterized by the cultivation of virtues such as wisdom, courage, justice, and temperance. While nowadays people may use the term "stoic" to refer to someone who is unemotional, true Stoicism (with a capital S) requires emotional intelligence and resilience. A Stoic is in touch with their feelings, but chooses to act wisely instead of impulsively. Learning to do this takes practice, as this is a philosophy that must not only be learned but also lived.

In this workbook, we cover the essentials of what Stoicism is and how to use this philosophy to live a meaningful and resilient life. We know that each day has its own stressors such as traffic, complainers, and setbacks. However, Marcus Aurelius reminds us that "the world is transformation, life is opinion" (*Meditations* 4.3). In other words, although the world and our personal environment may change, for better or worse, we can choose how we perceive things. We have the power to maintain inner peace and a sense of tranquility even amid unpeaceful times. Being Stoic doesn't mean turning a blind eye to injustice; it's also a philosophy of taking action. This stance is highly compatible with modern principles such as radical acceptance. A Stoic perspective allows us to reduce unnecessary suffering so we can focus our energies on what matters most.

How Stoic Are You Now?

You may be closer than you think. There may have been experiences in your life that have helped you become more inoculated to certain stresses. Before you delve further into this book and Stoic principles, let's find out how Stoic you already are, by taking the Stoicism self-inventory. You might want to do some of these worksheets more than once. You'll find PDF copies of many of the worksheets as well as bonus materials at the website for this book: http://www.newharbinger. com/52663.

Stoicism Self-Inventory

For the following statements, rate yourself on a scale of 0 to 5, where 0 = disagree and 5 = agree.

1. If it's out of my control, I don't let it stress me.

2. I give the benefit of the doubt when I think I've been wronged.

3. I don't feel the need to formulate an opinion about everything.

4. Just because I feel a certain way doesn't make it true.

5. I'm unafraid to make decisions that are for the greater good, even if they're final.

6. I practice emotional awareness.

7. I take the time to see things in the grand scheme before I react.

Rating

25–35: Stoic with a capital S!

20–24: Almost there!

0–19: Novice

"Where can I find a man like Socrates?": The Origin of Stoicism

Zeno of Citium, a once wealthy Phoenician merchant, founded Stoicism after his own "bounce back" event. A storm at sea stripped him of his entire stock of rare, sought-after dye. He was shipwrecked and a broke nobody, back to square one and stuck in Athens. While roaming the streets, he came upon a bookseller and read the philosophy of Socrates, who would later be hailed as the "godfather" of Stoicism. Socrates's perspective on ethics and interpretation of events inspired him. And so he, as legend has it, asked the bookseller, "Where can I find a man like Socrates?" The bookseller then pointed to a man just outside the window, Crates of Thebes, a famous philosopher. Zeno studied with Crates for decades until starting his own school of philosophy called Stoicism. His classes and discussions were held at the Stoa Poikile, a painted porch in Athens. His followers became known as "Stoics." There's roughly a direct line of succession from Socrates to Zeno. Antisthenes was a student of Socrates and Diogenes the Cynic (and founder of Cynicism) learned from Antisthenes. And Crates of Thebes, who taught Zeno, learned from Diogenes. So, Socrates → Antisthenes → Diogenes the Cynic → Crates of Thebes → Zeno of Citium → Stoicism.

Drawing on the teachings of Socrates and other earlier philosophers, the Stoics produced a wealth of written works, though only fragments have survived. Over time, Stoicism spread from Greece to Rome, where it gained popularity among statesmen. Cicero, a Roman consul whose writings had a significant impact on legal and political theory, studied Stoicism in Athens, providing important insights into the philosophy.

Despite the loss of many early works, we have a substantial body of literature from three Stoic philosophers of the Roman imperial period: Seneca the Younger, Epictetus, and Marcus Aurelius. Seneca's letters and essays on Stoicism were written while he served as tutor and advisor to Emperor Nero. Epictetus, a former slave, became one of the most influential philosophy teachers in Roman history, and his *Discourses* and *Enchiridion* (Handbook) remain as testimony to his ideas. Marcus Aurelius, the Roman emperor, devoted his life to Stoicism, having studied the works of Epictetus. Aurelius's private notebook, *The Meditations*, continues to be widely read today as the most authoritative work on Stoicism.

Despite a period of almost five centuries of flourishing, Stoicism waned in popularity, only to experience a resurgence in modern times as the primary philosophical inspiration for cognitive therapy, a widely practiced, evidence-based form of psychotherapy. Epictetus said what would become the cornerstone of both Stoicism and cognitive behavioral therapy in his *Enchiridion*: "It is not the event itself that disturbs us, but rather our own judgments about it" (*Enchiridion* 5).

Lowercase s Stoicism

Trading in emotional pain for a stiff upper lip is often culturally influenced. Emotion suppression is all too often considered courageous when it's actually a practice of utmost avoidance. What's become known as "toxic positivity" today is a form of lowercase *s* stoicism by avoiding negative emotion at all costs. The "good vibes only" narrative suppresses and pressurizes negative emotion within us, where it festers and causes lifelong distress.

True Stoicism doesn't aim for an emotionless life where we're disconnected from everything and feel nothing. In fact, the ancient Stoics wouldn't be in favor of this approach at all. Rather, the ability to not act on snap judgments or initial potentially erroneous impressions is the point. The ability to feel your feelings but not be controlled by them is the goal. The journey to building a life of lasting fulfillment is paved in this awareness, this ability, and its name is resilience.

The Relationship Between Stoicism and Cognitive Behavioral Therapy (CBT)

The father of cognitive behavioral therapy (CBT), Albert Ellis, was profoundly influenced by the Stoics. He too believed that we're ultimately responsible for the way we feel about a situation, and those feelings guide our decision making. This allots us the freedom and clarity to decide what we value and what deserves our emotional investment. CBT turns Stoic practices into modern and accessible tools to be applied to everyday modern life.

CBT, like society, has evolved over time. Initially, it focused on behavior modification and observable processes. The "cognitive revolution" introduced the importance of publicly unobservable thoughts and self-talk. Figures like Albert Ellis and Aaron Beck integrated cognitive strategies compatible with Stoic thought. Later, a third wave of CBT emphasized mindfulness and acceptance, focusing on living well by accepting feelings, choosing values, and taking action.

Philosophy is simply considered a framework to our outlook. It's really just the lens each of us views the world through, an approach to life. This book was written to help you apply this ancient wisdom to your life by offering an empowering lens from which to view it.

Stoicism is a philosophy and a way of life. Cognitive behavioral therapy offers resilience-building tools and exercises heavily inspired by Stoicism. However, these cognitive and behavioral tools only work if they continue to be used. Without consistent practice, it's easy to fall into old unhealthy emotional patterns and find yourself struggling, with unfortunate events once again perceived as catastrophes. Stoicism goes beyond using self-help techniques and instead asks you to adopt a set of ethical values and consistently live in accordance with them. This ancient philosophy has the potential to serve as a framework for attaining coping skills similar to those offered by CBT on a permanent basis.

Aaron Beck explained how his developing approach to therapy was based on the agreement among researchers that our thoughts have a significant impact on our emotions: "Nevertheless, the philosophical underpinnings go back thousands of years, certainly to the time of the Stoics, who considered man's conceptions (or misconceptions) of events rather than the events themselves as the key to his emotional upsets" (Beck 1976, 3).

Stoicism suggests that focusing on virtue and our personal values—what's most important to the whole of our life—keeps us from falling into despair when we face adversity. After all, what is it to give up on life but to lose perspective of what genuinely matters to us in the grand scheme? We will help you clarify your values, as well as offer an overview of each of the Stoic virtues (wisdom, justice, courage, temperance), in chapter 3. For now, let's look at the example of Lee in the following story.

Lee's home renovation manufacturing company is going through dark times right now. Budget cuts have led to mass layoffs and, unfortunately, he was told that his position was being eliminated. He'd been a loyal employee for nearly ten years, had a good pension plan, and was looking forward to his kids reaping the benefits of the company dependent scholarship program. However, in that moment, in that cold sterile office, he feels a hit to his pension, opportunity being ripped from his children, and his ten-year loyalty meaningless. He looks to the ceiling and sighs as his manager offers his sincere condolences. In that moment, his mind is divided between a snarky obscenities-filled response or a strong and silent exit. Suppressing both potential responses feels as if he is holding his breath underwater.

Is there a third option for Lee? One where he doesn't feel stifled or ingenuine?

Lee tries to shove his anger deep down, only to feel it pressurize. But before it launches out of him, he takes a moment that may mean all the difference to his future. "I must admit, I'm shocked and disappointed by this news," he says, semi-relieved at his own transparency. "I do acknowledge that this decision wasn't up to you, though, and I appreciate having been given the opportunity to work for this company." He knows he will never be entirely sure that his response is the perfect one. He knows it is the best one, though. Because he values integrity and honesty, he knows this is a response that he can walk away feeling okay with.

As we touched on earlier, resilience is the ability to adapt to difficult or challenging life experiences, whether internal or external, controllable or uncontrollable. Let's take a minute to examine the predicament Lee finds himself in.

What could Lee control about what just happened? Well, the long and short answer is nothing. He has no control over the decisions that were made for him by a company that was experiencing losses. It's not as if his performance, which is in his control, had any influence over the decision. Last year's losses were not down to a single employee no matter how valuable they were. It would be wildly illogical to think otherwise.

What does he have control over now? While he doesn't have control over the past, he does have control over what he does with that past, full of experience, company milestones, and positive yearly reviews. Lee realizes he has five years' experience being a systems analyst, and the severance pay will buy him some time. Remembering that he always wished he had the benefits package his cousin had, but was too scared to leave the company, Lee realizes he now has options…and nothing to lose.

Stoicism isn't looking for silver linings in bad situations, but rather focusing on what you have control over and making wise decisions. The emotional toll of losing the job is real, and Lee feels it. At the same time, he's focused on moving forward. The things that made him attractive to this job will make him attractive to another one, and now he has even more experience. This transition will be difficult, but he'll make it through.

What does Lee have control over in the situation?

_____

_____

_____

_____

What are the things that have already happened that are out of his control?

_____

_____

_____

_____

What are the pitfalls that could get Lee stuck?

_____

_____

_____

_____

What's the most important thing for him to focus on right now?

_____

_____

_____

_____

What steps should he take to accomplish that?

_____

_____

_____

_____

Lee is an interpersonal example of resilience. Resilience comes in many forms. Beyond how we respond or how resilience allows us to reframe a situation, resilience can be exemplified in times of grief or by an entire city determined to rebuild after a devastating tornado. Resilience is feeling the impact but redirecting our initial feelings in efforts to press on and thrive anyway. The crucial part of that process is first taking inventory of what we can control and what we can't about the situation. This offers clarity and acts as a preventive measure against self-blame and further purposeless grief that fuels spiraling.

What Is Resilience?

Being resilient isn't simply being "strong and silent," having a "stiff upper lip," or preserving an "onward march" about things. This, unfortunately, is how resilience is understood in the minds of many.

What does resilience mean to me?

_____

_____

_____

_____

_____

_____

Martin Seligman, a renowned psychologist, defines resilience as the ability to overcome adversity and continue functioning in a positive and productive manner. In his work on positive psychology, Seligman emphasizes that resilience isn't simply the absence of negative emotions or experiences, but rather the presence of positive emotions and a capacity for growth and adaptation in the face of challenges.

When it comes to resilience, flexibility is key. Housebuilders use nails instead of screws, because nails are flexible and allow the home some ability to shift with the weather and ground movements. Screws, on the other hand, can't bend, so they break. Similarly, the willow tree is hardy because it's flexible and has deep, vigorous roots. A windstorm might bring down an oak tree but the willow will remain standing.

Resilience is, in fact, the ability to adapt to difficult or challenging life experiences by adopting a practice and viewpoint that is psychologically flexible. It's the ability to bounce back from a tough time, not force a smile through the hurt.

Why Resilience Matters

Adversity takes many forms, as does resilience. Whether a person lets you down or you miss an opportunity, being disappointed is a natural occurrence in life, and we're all in this together. From a death in the family to a tornado tearing through a community, no one is exempt from misfortune. Lacking the ability to cope and move on and thrive after these life stressors contributes largely to the development of mental illness. For those with limited resilience, stressful events become debilitating. People who have a healthy amount of resilience, however, bear inner resources they instinctively tap into during difficult times, resulting in lower levels of anxiety and depression.

The great news is that although some of us didn't grow up in an environment that fostered healthy coping skills, resilience can still be acquired! A study from the Resilience Institute shows that those who performed resilience-building exercises experienced a reduction in their depressive symptoms by 33 to 44 percent. Participants also found their overall well-being improved: physical (43 percent), emotional (40 percent), and mental (38 percent). Working toward resilience could mean the difference between being debilitated by adverse events and moving on, flourishing despite the pain.

What are my reasons for trying out this workbook?

_____

_____

_____

_____

Do I have specific things I'm hoping to learn?

_____

_____

_____

_____

Do I have specific problems I want to address?

_____

_____

_____

_____

Do I have goals or ambitions I want to work toward?

_____

_____

_____

_____

Even a goal of simply wanting to stimulate your mind or enlarge your understanding of either Stoicism or cognitive behavioral therapy is a worthy goal. If you clarify your ambition, you can approach each exercise with purpose and intention. And, sometimes what you hoped to get out of something changes along the way.

First, delineate things that are accomplishable (goals) and things that are continually ongoing (values and virtues). For example, if you have a value of being a good parent, this isn't something that can be completed with a single short- or long-term goal. One of the hardest things about being a good parent is that it takes persistent effort. In the movies, grand gestures are what it takes to have a good relationship, but in real life it's often the constant little things that matter most. Developing the discipline for persistent effort toward what you value most is at the core of Stoicism. What's currently often called "values" is what early Stoics would have called "virtues." The four core Stoic virtues are wisdom, justice, courage, and temperance. These values inform the contents of this workbook.

Though it's up to you to choose what you will value most in life, if you're leaning toward saying that you value an absence of pain or discomfort, you might take it a step further and ask what you would want instead. For example, if a large amount of your time and energy goes into being socially anxious, what would you want to do with that time and energy instead? The thing you would rather do instead is what you value, and the anxiety would be a barrier to overcome. Use the following exercise to take a moment and ask yourself: "What do I want my life to be like?" and "What's getting in the way of that?" Remember also that this is your own personal assessment, only for you. So, don't feel that you should answer according to what someone else thinks is the "right" kind of life you should lead, what your parents or society would want. What do *you* want your life to be like?

What values am I working toward? (What do I want?)	What are the barriers to those goals? (What's getting in the way?)

Chapter 1 Takeaways

- Stoicism involves emotional resilience as opposed to suppression of emotion.

- Resilience is an adoptable ability.

- To be resilient is to possess the psychological flexibility to adapt to adversity.

- "It is not events that disturb us, but rather our judgments about them."

- This workbook will focus on using ancient and modern wisdom to help you live a fulfilling life.

CHAPTER 2

The Paradox of Control and Stoic Practices to Embrace Not Having It

Some things are in our control and others not. Things in our control are opinion, what we choose to pursue, our desires, aversions, and, put simply, our own deeds. Things not in our control are body, property, reputation, command, and whatever happens that is not of our own doing.

—Epictetus, *Enchiridion* 1

The paradox of control is the pitfall of trying to control the uncontrollable and investing all our efforts in that belief. This leads to a significant amount of time lost to attempts at influencing outcomes we can't, which historically results in the loss of governance over our own thoughts, emotions, and actions. The *dichotomy of control*, its antithesis, is a philosophical concept introduced by Epictetus that's quite often applied in modern-day therapy. It refers to the division of things in our lives into two categories: those that are within our control and those that are not. In fact, Epictetus opens the *Enchiridion* with this fact of life: "Some things are up to us, others are not."

Is traffic frustrating? Of course it is. Can we part the sea of cars with our minds? Unfortunately, no. When we miss a flight, can we chase it down the runway and grab onto the wing? No, that's both illegal and highly dangerous. Is it possible to hop in a time machine and prevent saying that embarrassing, cringe-worthy thing you said to your crush in eleventh grade? Not currently anyway. Lastly, does anxiety about the future change it? While there are productive things we can do to *influence* it, life happens as it will. These all sound like ridiculous questions, but if there's nothing we can do about something we can't directly control, then isn't worrying about it just as ludicrous?

It isn't surprising that the grand majority of our distress comes from worrying about what we have no control over. Author and psychotherapist Tim LeBon noted this common denominator in his clients spanning over a decade in his book *365 Ways to Be More Stoic*:

"As a psychotherapist, the more I read about Stoicism, the more I realized this ancient philosophy is incredibly relatable to my modern-day clients. Going back through my caseload, I see many problems lead back to the same root cause: trying to control the uncontrollable.

Anger and frustration—*believing you can control other people*

Shame and guilt—*believing you had more control over the past*

Worry and anxiety—*overthinking aspects of the future you can't control*

Procrastination—*trying to get everything perfect before you start—you can't make everything perfect*" (LeBon 2022, 13).

What we do have control over is conveyed in Epictetus's line that opens this chapter: our opinions, desires, deeds…put simply, our own thoughts and actions. That's it. To think otherwise is to go against logic, expending mental and emotional energy, which can be a waste of time and resources. Breaking things down can help you see which parts of a situation are within your control. For example, you might not be able to control your initial reaction to an event, but you can control how you choose to respond to it.

The Stoic archer is a common analogy Stoicism offers in support of the dichotomy of control. Archery is all in the form: the stance, aim, and release. After the archer has released the arrow, they have no control over how externals (like the wind) affect the arrow's flight and where it lands. In fact, they have no control whatsoever after the arrow takes flight. As Epictetus wrote, "Rather than striving to make events unfold according to your desires, embrace them as they naturally occur. If you can do this, you will find contentment" (*Enchiridion* 8). You can find a downloadable copy of the following exercise at http://www.newharbinger.com/52663.

Pick something you're currently worried about. Break down that situation into its components. Next, sort these pieces of the situation by whether they're under your direct control. Repeat this process with the worries that come up for you during the week.

What's Under My Control?		
Situation	Can Control (✓)	Can't Control (✓)

What do I notice about the pattern?

_____

_____

_____

_____

What did I learn about myself?

_____

_____

_____

_____

What types of things that are out of my control do I tend to focus on the most?

_____

_____

_____

Based on this information, what do I want to do?

_____

_____

_____

_____

Why Do We Want Control?

There could be numerous situation-specific reasons as to why we feel we must be in control. However, most everything on that list falls under the umbrella of the fear of *uncertainty*. It's an innate desire to want to feel safe. "Unsafe" and "uncertain" are related but distinct concepts. Something that's unsafe is potentially harmful or dangerous, while something that's uncertain isn't known or not certain to happen. Specifically, "unsafe" refers to the potential for harm, while "uncertain" refers to the lack of information or predictability. For example, driving a car with faulty brakes is unsafe because there's a risk of getting into an accident, whereas not knowing the outcome of a sports game is uncertain because the result isn't yet known.

Fear is a signal for survival, and irrational fear is a fear of that which isn't most likely. The truth is, we can worry all we want, but it will never grant us certainty of anything. Whatever happens, if you've done all you could, embrace the uncertainty of life. Without exception, hardships and bad things will happen to everyone; indeed, truly terrible things that are out of your control might happen. The great majority of the time (if not always), it isn't something you won't be able to bounce back from. The cliché is that whatever doesn't kill you makes you stronger. The Stoics might instead say, "You can't control what happens to you, but you can control how you respond to it." You can actively choose to heal and overcome. A setback doesn't have to become a permanent blockage. In everything there's opportunity.

The need for control drives humans to often have an intolerance of uncertainty. Many people would rather have "bad news" than "no news." Many people try to cheat uncertainty by mentally running through every hypothetical scenario of what could happen so they won't be caught off guard. But what are the costs of not tolerating some uncertainty in your life?

How often do I worry and obsess about what *could* happen?

_____

_____

_____

_____

Does worrying about what *could* happen distract me from being present in what's *actually* happening in my life? How?

_____

_____

_____

_____

How does that affect my job, relationships, leisure, and so on?

_____

_____

_____

Do I avoid relationships, activities, outings, and other endeavors because I worry too much about what might happen?

_____

_____

_____

What have I already missed out on because of this?

_____

_____

_____

The surest way to avoid uncertainty is to create a life that's small and boring. Given the choice between a life that's small with minimal uncertainty or a life that's full of meaning and adventure (including all the good and bad that comes with it), which would I choose? Why?

_____

_____

_____

_____

How does my relationship with uncertainty affect my choice?

_____

_____

_____

_____

Don't Worry 'Bout It!: Being Indifferent to What Makes No Difference

We all prefer to be alleviated from anxiety. Most of us would like to care a little less about the things that disturb us, so we can spend more time focused on what serves us. Moreover, we would all like to have a calm mind and feelings of peace and contentment.

First, what's indifference? It's that which is neither good nor bad, but that which doesn't make any difference to our inner state and shouldn't matter in the grand scheme. The Stoics divide indifference into two categories: preferred and dispreferred indifferents. A *preferred* indifferent is an external circumstance or condition that we might desire, but that shouldn't determine our happiness or self-worth. These are things like strength, wealth, pleasure, and social status. The Stoics believed that we should aim to take these things off their pedestal and take a stance of indifference toward them. That's also because these things aren't necessarily in our control, as supported by Epictetus, when he said, "Our body, property, reputation, authority, and essentially anything that's not the result of our own actions are beyond our control" (Epictetus, *Enchiridion* 1). Just like the Stoic archer, we can aim to be rich, but if our arrow is thrown off course, are we then doomed to a life of misery? Do our lives lose meaning if we're not driving a Porsche on the way to some swanky party in Beverly Hills? The point is, why should being wealthy matter over the lasting peace that comes with being content? When we say *content*, we don't mean settling for what is. That means to be complacent, to settle for things that aren't good for us or less than desirable conditions. To be content, on the other hand, is to appreciate and accept where we are. Our present condition doesn't have to be a final stop, but resenting our environment isn't a constructive method of ever leaving it.

When it comes to having social standing, we only have so much control over the perception of others. We can influence and should strive to be our authentic, best selves. Not everyone will choose to take that view of you, though. It's a fact of life that not everyone will like you. Having that be our goal is another way we keep up the never-ending chase for happiness.

A *dispreferred* indifferent is another external circumstance or desire. However, it's dispreferred because we would rather not have it befall us if we were given the choice, such as disease, weakness, ugliness, poverty, and a lowly reputation. Even our health can be considered a dispreferred indifferent. We should all prefer to be healthy. Although we should strive to take optimum care of ourselves, none of us is exempt from illnesses—even if we try our hardest to prevent them. We will all get progressively ill as we enter old age. We may naturally deny and grieve this fate, but the graceful acceptance of it over time provides peace. Wisdom comes from knowing that we all eventually return to nature.

When it comes to our looks, we of course would prefer to look gorgeous, but we all have different definitions of beauty. The fact is, no matter how beautiful we make ourselves, beauty fades. The best plastic surgeons in the world can work wonders, but even those wonders can't defy the inevitable aging process. Marcus Aurelius offers this in support of the fact that we will all wrinkle and fade away, saying, "Life is short. All of us started out as a blob of semen. Soon enough, we will become ash. This is nature and we are just passing through" (*Meditations* 4.48). We can alter our fleshy shells all we want. But to focus on that and only that is to, again, chase down the speeding train to happiness that never meets its destination. Even those who feel they have achieved the look they want are not exempt from unhappiness. If their look is their main achievement, soon they will be looking for an update. Because they aren't living in accordance with their values—what means most to them aside from simply lookin' good—they may be miserable until they have it. Then the cycle of beauty-pain-beauty-pain will lead them to, you guessed it, *misery*.

Identifying the things that should make no difference in our lives frees us from considering them as having control over our happiness or state of flourishing. We can choose to dethrone these invaluable externals and keep a calm mind should they show up in our lives. Having a calm mind contributes to our ability to make decisions, offering some assurance that we will be okay regardless. Cicero's attributed maxim, "Peace is liberty in tranquility," elegantly encapsulates the profound essence of this sentiment.

Review the following list and sort items into things that people care about and things that actually matter.

Item	Things that people care about (✓)	Things that actually matter (✓)
How you treat other people		
How many followers you have on social media		
How green your lawn is		
Your dress size		
Being in good health		

Next, make a list of some of the things that the people in your life care about and then sort those into things that people care about and things that actually matter

Item	Things that people care about (✓)	Things that actually matter (✓)

Fate Permitting ("God Willing")

The Stoics didn't believe in a personal god or deity in the way that many religions do. Instead, they believed in a divine force or power that governed the universe, and they saw this power as immanent rather than transcendent. Therefore, when the Stoics said "god willing," they were not referring to a personal god who had the ability to intervene in human affairs. Instead, they were expressing the idea that the events of our life are ultimately determined by the will of this divine power, and that it is up to each individual to align themselves with this power and to live in accordance with its laws.

The Delphic Maxims are a set of maxims inscribed on the Temple of Apollo at Delphi that are simple statements offering advice on how to live a good and fulfilling life. One of the maxims is *amor fati* (τύχην στέργε), which means "love your fate." The exact wording of the maxim varies, but it's generally understood to mean that we shouldn't try to second-guess or attempt to control fate, but rather accept the course of events as they unfold and make the most of the opportunities that present themselves. This idea is often expressed in the phrase "fate permitting" or "if fate permits." So, it's more reasonable to say "fate permitting" rather than "god willing": "I'll be there, fate permitting," "I'll reach this goal, fate permitting," and so on. This is otherwise known as adding a *reserve clause*, a clause that reminds us that not everything in our lives will go according to plan.

In alignment with the value of letting go of our attachments, it's beneficial to consider *everything* in the context of "fate permitting." By adding a reserve clause, we reframe how we view things that we plan on happening. It also helps us develop resilience and be more adaptable to change, as it reminds us that life is constantly changing and we must be prepared for the unexpected—like a car accident or having double-booked an event. This way, we're not inclined to be so hard on ourselves when these things occur.

You can only do *anything* if fate permits it. Self-deprecating thoughts when we blame ourselves for what we could not control leads to low self-esteem, self-doubt, and feelings of inadequacy or worthlessness. Over time, they can contribute to a cycle of negative thinking and make it difficult to believe in ourselves and pursue our goals. They can also interfere with our ability to form and maintain healthy relationships, leaving us with feelings of loneliness and isolation. In severe cases, self-deprecating thoughts can contribute to the development of depression or anxiety. This is why getting in the practice of adding "fate permitting" to anything we commit to, verbally or mentally, is so valuable.

"We can't direct the wind, but we can adjust the sails" is an old proverb that reinforces the idea of "fate permitting." We can only do our best and control what's within our power to control with the information that's available to us. We hope you're not too hard on yourself, fate permitting, and that this book has landed in the hands of someone who can really benefit, fate permitting.

Can the Worry Before It Cans You

Homer Simpson is great at exemplifying human behavior that's both innate and strange. In one particular episode of *The Simpsons*, he purchases a soda from a vending machine only for it to get stuck on the way out. He then reaches his arm up into the machine and gets "stuck." After several attempts to get his arm out, crew members arrive at a point where they may have to cut his arm off. Then one of them asks the golden question, "Homer, are you just holding on to the can?"

It's the same with our worry: we're only stuck because we're making that choice. We feel if we're not in control, we're out of control, even when the control we think we have is just an illusion. It's the can we clutch to desperately like an amulet that will protect us. Really, it's far from an amulet and more like a pet rock: just hard and useless. Yet, we often feel that worrying about the uncontrollable allows us to take action and do something to protect ourselves, performing some sort of damage control. We are, in fact, doing something, just not anything positive.

Many of us take on the perception that if we're not in control, we're out of control; in fact, it's quite the opposite. Gripping firmly to our worry puts a tight lid on our potential. It can interfere with our ability to focus and concentrate on the task at hand. When we're in a consistent state of worry, we often have racing thoughts and are preoccupied with potential problems or unfavorable outcomes. This can make it difficult for us to pay attention to what we're doing and to think clearly. As a result, we may make blunders or fail to perform at our best. Then we worry that we've lost the best part of ourselves and question our skills even if we've proven them before.

If we let worry fester, anxiety and fear become the platform from which we make decisions, rather than logic or evidence. As a result, we may make choices that are not in our best interests or that are not aligned with our values and goals. We may avoid taking risks or trying new things out of fear of failure or rejection. Additionally, we may avoid seeking help or support when we need it, or we may engage in unhealthy behaviors, such as excessive alcohol or drug use, in an attempt to cope with our worry.

Being committed to worry also leaves us feeling unhappy and dissatisfied, and it destroys how we view the world in which we live. Instead of seeing the compassion, empathy, honesty, and respect people express, we only see the worrisome behavior, like hate, disrespect, and selfishness. This can cause us to take a pessimistic stance on most everything in life, and it can interfere with our current relationships or prevent new ones from forming. Over time, this can lead us to develop a distorted or unhealthy worldview that's based on fear and anxiety, rather than on a positive and realistic perspective.

In short, worrying isn't damage control; rather, it's worrying about what we can't control that damages and controls us. It's like thinking we're in a standoff with the negative when, really, worry is just us versus us; we become our own worst enemy. This is why it's so important to let go of worry and focus on the things that we can control, lest worry control our lives. This can help us maintain a healthy worldview, keeping us efficient and actively living in the present, improving our overall well-being. As Marcus Aurelius (2003) put it, "Your own happiness depends on the standard of your thoughts."

Here's a good analogy that's similar to Homer Simpson's predicament: There's a certain kind of trap that works really well on monkeys. Trappers drill a small hole in a coconut and fill it with a treat. The monkey reaches in to grab the treat but upon retraction, its hand gets stuck. This is because a full hand is larger than an empty hand and wider than the opening (see figure 1). The monkey could be free, if it would only let go. You can find a downloadable copy of the following exercise at http://www.newharbinger.com/52663.

Escaping the Monkey Trap

What's something I won't let go of that's keeping me stuck?

_____

_____

What would I lose if I let go?

_____

_____

_____

What would I gain if I allowed myself to let go?

_____

_____

Which do I want more: my freedom or an unachievable outcome?

_____

_____

_____

Become Tolerant of Uncertainty

To conclude this chapter, we will leave you with the task of challenging your own intolerance of uncertainty. Accepting and embracing uncertainty takes time. Remember, uncertainty is a natural part of life, and not something to be feared or avoided. Instead, it's an opportunity to learn, grow, and thrive. Just as a surfer must adapt to the changing conditions of the ocean, we must adapt to the unpredictable and ever-changing events of our lives. We can't control the waves, but we can learn to ride them no matter how big or small, to find balance and harmony. Surfers have a lot of fun riding those waves, so why shouldn't we? Embracing uncertainty and learning to ride the waves of life helps us find meaning and fulfillment in our experiences, no matter what they may bring. Here are some questions to ask yourself daily in efforts to embrace uncertainty in the long term:

- Is it possible to be certain of everything in my life?

- How is my need for certainty helpful or unhelpful?

- Is it reasonable to predict that bad things will happen just because I'm uncertain?

- What's the likelihood of good things happening versus bad things happening?

- How likely am I to predict the future?

- What advice would I give a good friend who is afraid of the unknown?

Chapter 2 Takeaways

- Divide events into categories of what you do and don't have control over.

- Suffering comes from trying to control what you can't.

- Impermanence unites us; no one gets out of here alive.

- Increasing tolerance of uncertainty increases resilience.

CHAPTER 3

Virtues and Values Clarification

First tell yourself what kind of person you want to be, then do what you have to do.

—Epictetus, *Discourses* 3.23

The ancient Stoic philosophers believed in living in accordance with four virtues: wisdom, justice, courage, and temperance. Wisdom, one could say, is knowing what's most important to us in life. Modalities like acceptance and commitment therapy place a significant emphasis on the concept of values. When we talk about values in this context, we're referring to the characteristics of behavior that are essential to us and provide a sense of fulfillment. They're the things that we genuinely aspire to do in life and the kind of person we strive to be. You can find a downloadable copy of the following exercise at http://www.newharbinger.com/52663.

A first step in clarifying your values is identifying things you're doing (or think you ought to be doing) and ask yourself the following questions:

Why does this matter to me?

_____

_____

_____

_____

_____

Am I doing this because it's in line with who I want to be? How so?

_____

_____

_____

_____

_____

Or am I doing this to avoid feeling discomfort? How so?

_____

_____

_____

_____

_____

Moving Away from Values	Moving Toward Values
What am I trying to avoid?	What are my priorities?
What makes me uncomfortable?	What matters to me?
What am I missing out on?	What do I want to do with my life?

After filling in the chart, reflect on the following questions:

If by some miracle I wasn't bothered by the discomfort, if the problems I worry about were magically gone, what would I want to prioritize in my life?

_____

_____

_____

_____

What do I learn from this about what matters to me?

_____

_____

_____

_____

There are things we do because they give our life meaning, and there are things we do to stay occupied so we're not alone with our thoughts and feelings. As author Tara Brach said, "Staying occupied is a socially sanctioned way of remaining distant from our pain" (Brach 2004, 16). Someone could be really into music because constantly listening to it distracts them from what's happening in their life. In a way, this constant listening to music might be a coping skill and in another way it's an avoidance. Now, if this interest in music is about more than escapism, then it might be in line with your values. Values are less about *what you do not want* and more about *what you do want*—specifically, what you want to *do*. What do you want to make important in your life? And how are you going to demonstrate that through your actions? Values give our life direction, and goals might be specific steps on that journey. If someone has an interest in music, they might have goals related to learning to play a specific song or go to a specific concert. These are clear objectives that can be fun to pursue, and there can be a dysphoria that follows goal comple-tion, the sense of, "Well, what do I have to look forward to now?"

In this chapter, we'll delve into the primary virtues outlined by the Stoics, as well as those espoused by Peterson and Seligman's (2004) methodology, which you'll read about shortly. We'll show you how to use uncomplicated questions to clarify your values. Lastly, we'll tackle one of the most prevalent issues in this domain: how to ensure that you're not merely embracing soci-ety's or other individuals' values but determining for yourself what constitutes a gratifying life.

Why Are Values and Virtues Important?

Another important question on the way to identifying what matters to us is asking ourselves, "What's the aim of the whole of my life?" A life spent chasing happiness is often unfulfilling, as happiness itself can be fleeting. Typically, to get what you want in life, you have to be able to tolerate and endure things that are unpleasant. If you view happiness as whether you're immedi-ately and continually feeling pleasure, you're susceptible to a host of self-defeating patterns and addictive behaviors. If you can mentally take a step back and view your experiences across your lifetime, there's perspective to be gained. The Stoics had a term for this pleasantness that comes with living a life of fulfillment and meaning: *eudaimonia* (or flourishing). This ultimate aim of life can only be achieved by consistently living in accordance with wisdom and the other virtues.

Flourishing brings to mind the imagery of vegetation experiencing vigorous and healthy growth. If you're a gardener, you know that if you want to see results, you need to put in constant effort and upkeep. While there are plenty of joys, there also can be backbreaking work. Success is viewed over time, and long-term fulfillment is what makes it worth it.

The Stoics and other Greek philosophers used the unique term *eudaimonia* to refer to the ultimate aim of life. Though notoriously difficult to translate, it literally means "having a good daemon," or a guiding spirit. In the past, it was commonly translated as "happiness," but most modern scholars agree that words like "flourishing" or "fulfillment" provide a better translation. Eudaimonia isn't merely a feeling; it's a complete state of being. It's the condition of a person who is living their best life, living well in the moments between the roars of the crowd. In the next exercise, you'll check whether the values you clarified at the start of the chapter are the ones you are truly living.

What are some of the goals and ambitions I have for my life?

_____

_____

_____

_____

In a hypothetical scenario where I did these things and didn't get to tell anyone I did them or post about them online, would this change which ones are most important to me?

_____

_____

_____

Are there things I want to do to be able to impress other people?

_____

_____

_____

_____

Are there areas I find myself seeking fulfillment through the external validation of others?

_____

_____

_____

_____

What kind of life do I want for myself?

_____

_____

_____

What would give personal meaning to my life?

_____

_____

_____

Are there activities I do to impress/please other people that don't align with who I want to be?

_____

_____

_____

What do I want to prioritize?

_____

_____

_____

On a scale of 0 to 10, where 0 = not at all and 10 = completely, rate how much each of these virtues matters to you.

Wisdom: _____   Justice: _____

Courage: _____   Temperance: _____

How have I seen other people demonstrate these virtues in their lives?

Wisdom: _____

_____

Justice: _____

_____

Courage: _____

_____

Temperance: _____

_____

Are there any areas I want to work on?

_____

_____

Wisdom

While others may prioritize things like wealth and reputation, the Stoics recognized that these things are not as important as they may appear. Ignorance or foolishness, on the other hand, involves thinking about our lives irrationally and being misled by what we see on the surface. For the Stoics, wisdom involves recognizing that external advantages are less important than how we use them, and that using them effectively requires reason and good judgment. In fact, Stoic wisdom is intentionally self-referential, as it values and studies itself above all else.

It's impossible to exercise the other virtues without utilizing wisdom. The best way to know whether something is good or not, right or wrong, is to project ourselves into the future. Acknowledge that it may seem difficult but also ask yourself, *Is this going to be good for me in the long run?* Wisdom also enables us to see things as they really are, rather than being swayed by our emotions or preconceived notions.

Describe a recent interpersonal interaction that didn't go how I wanted it to.

_____

_____

_____

_____

What was happening in that situation?

_____

_____

_____

What elements of that situation were under my control?

_____

_____

_____

What was the outcome I wanted in that situation?

_____

_____

_____

_____

Is what I wanted realistic?

_____

_____

_____

Within the limits of what was under my control, what would I have had to do to get what I wanted?

_____

_____

_____

_____

What did I learn from this activity that can be applied to future interactions?

_____

_____

_____

_____

_____

Wisdom Is a Skill

It isn't a wonder that the paragon of wisdom, Socrates, would exemplify many examples of wisdom in action. Interestingly, a dialogue Socrates had with Meno, a young nobleman, exemplified his thoughts on the nature of virtue. Meno begins by asking Socrates what virtue is and whether it's something that can be taught. Initiating the Socratic Method, Socrates asks him to define "virtue." While Socrates and Meno attempt to define virtue, they find it challenging. Although they don't arrive at a specific definition, they both gained valuable insights and perspectives that revealed the limits of their knowledge. The dialogue served to stimulate their thinking, challenge their assumptions, and demonstrate the value of open inquiry. The conversation itself, as well as the insights gained from it, are reflective of the broader aims of Socratic philosophy: gaining wisdom by overcoming ignorance. Wisdom itself is thus a process and a skill.

Justice

Wisdom, when applied to our relationships with others, leads to what the ancient Greeks called *dikaiosune*. This word translates as "justice," but the meaning is broader than how we think of the word. It would be better translated to us as "social virtue." The Stoics divide this into "fairness" and "kindness."

The part of social virtue we know as "justice," or "fairness," the Stoics sometimes defined as showing others the respect they deserve, treating them fairly. Today's readers often point out that there's a great deal of disagreement about what justice looks like in practice. It's a complex subject with endless books trying to explain it. Fortunately, there's a well-known, centuries-old rule adopted by different religions and philosophies, including Stoicism: the "Golden Rule." It says, broadly speaking, that we should treat other people with the same respect that we would like to receive from them—or *do unto others as we would have them do unto us*, as the Bible puts it. The corresponding vice, injustice or unfairness, consists in exploiting others, treating them with disrespect, and not giving them their due.

Kindness and Compassion

Kindness has always been an essential aspect of social virtue. It involves wishing for the well-being of others, both individually and collectively, and treating them as friends rather than enemies. The Stoic emperor Marcus Aurelius, for instance, constructed a temple to "Beneficence," which represents the act of helping others. Although the happiness of others isn't entirely within our control, the Stoics don't remain indifferent to their flourishing and wish for their success, acknowledging that fate also plays a role. The opposite of kindness is cruelty or anger, which the Stoics define as the desire for others to suffer. Overcoming anger and replacing it with kindness or compassion is one of the primary objectives of ancient Stoic therapy.

For the Stoics, helping others goes beyond providing them with material assistance. To demonstrate wisdom in helping others, we must examine fundamental questions such as "What's good for us?" and "What does it mean to help or harm someone?" Despite the apparent importance that society places on wealth and reputation, the Stoics believe that wisdom or virtue is the only genuine good. Thus, educating or sharing wisdom with others is a more valuable form of assistance than providing external advantages. Although kindness and compassion are typically regarded as virtues that we demonstrate in relation to others, the Stoics also view philosophy as a means of cultivating self-friendship, or self-compassion.

What were things I needed but didn't receive during the formative years of my life?

_____

_____

_____

_____

For better or worse, how did those experiences affect who I am today?

_____

_____

_____

_____

Can I offer some compassion to myself, as I see the context of my history?

_____

_____

_____

_____

How can I offer myself *now* what I needed *then?*

_____

_____

_____

_____

_____

Courage

Fear is one of our greatest survival instincts. This feeling is an innate signal that something could be harmful to us. When it becomes more than that, though, fear doesn't make us inadequate but rather prevents us from doing what's necessary and good. There are times in our lives when we feel the need to speak up or act against injustices, but we're afraid because of what others may think of us. *Courage* is feeling the fear but doing it anyway. Fearing anything that doesn't pertain to a life-or-death situation could be classified as an *irrational* fear. As Marcus Aurelius said, "Only if it ruins your character does it ruin your life. If it doesn't, then you are impermeable to it. It can't harm you" (*Meditations* 4.8).

It would be more damaging to your character if you chose to not speak up or act. And your character shouldn't be left to be determined by those who think you're a fool for speaking out against injustices. Besides, even if they do think this of you, still, nothing terrible has happened to you.

Courage can also mean being steadfast in your manner, unfazed in a crisis when leading a team or even your family. If you're in such a leadership role, people look to you to be their rock. This doesn't mean being void of fear, but not making it worse by exaggerating the magnitude of the crisis. Catastrophizing is counterproductive. It takes courage to not let fear get in the way of rightful decision making. In many situations, people who struggle with fear and anxiety have learned to be intolerant of feeling anxious. "I just can't stand feeling this way" is something they might say. They often develop a fear of fear itself. This is what the Stoics mean when they speak of courage.

Was there ever a time I was afraid to do something and I had to do it anyway?

_____

_____

_____

_____

What about the situation was scary?

_____

_____

_____

What happened in that situation?

_____

_____

_____

Did I do what had to be done despite feeling anxious?

_____

_____

_____

Have I surprised myself by doing things I doubted I could do?

_____

_____

_____

Is it possible for me to feel fear and do challenging things anyway?

_____

_____

_____

What are some of the fears I've had to face in my life?

_____

_____

_____

_____

What are some of the fears I still need to face in my life?

_____

_____

_____

_____

Are there things that are scary (but not dangerous) that I can practice to cultivate my ability to act with courage?

_____

_____

_____

_____

Temperance

When it comes to *temperance*, we could simply say it's the ability to maintain self-control, but it's also understanding what influences our cravings, such as genetics, environment, emotions, and social norms. By understanding our underlying unhealthy desires, we can develop strategies to manage them and make healthier choices. Marcus Aurelius's advice is to seek to extinguish the appetite: "Wipe out distractions, manage your desires, and extinguish unhealthy cravings, and you will maintain power over your mind as well as your decisions" (*Meditations* 2.5).

To extinguish unhealthy cravings, and not simply quench them, we must understand their source. When it comes down to it, our yearnings are fueled by their context. To understand these contexts is an act of wisdom, delving further into knowing thyself.

According to the Stoics, people suffer because they excessively desire things like fame, wealth, sex, food, drink, or other pleasures, which can lead to addiction. Someone who demonstrates moderation is able to renounce unhealthy desires and resist the craving for certain pleasures that may feel good but are not beneficial. However, moderation alone isn't a virtue unless it's accompanied by wisdom, as self-discipline without discernment can lead to damaging behavior. True moderation requires understanding what's appropriate to desire and what to renounce, and this knowledge is gained through self-awareness.

The opposite of temperance is intemperance, or excess, which is characterized by self-indulgence and a lack of restraint. Socrates and the Stoics believed that wisdom without temperance was meaningless, as it leaves us vulnerable to temptation and poor decision making. To overcome irrational or unhealthy desires and habits, therapy and self-help are often necessary. The ancient

Greek saying "Nothing in excess" emphasizes the importance of balance and moderation, a central theme in ancient philosophy.

It isn't just cravings but controlling our temper that temperance encompasses as well. Like our indulgences, the Stoics contemplate the consequences of bursting into a fit of rage. The Stoics also believe that anger does more harm to us than good. Stoic philosopher Seneca deemed anger as a "temporary madness" in his work *On Anger*. We're in a fit of madness because we've become someone else, and we do things that an otherwise sane (and wise) person wouldn't. When anger comes on, it comes on *fast*. Even if you're slower to it, anger can still build a murky plaque over how we feel about things we once enjoyed. Do you really hate your job, or did you just have a bad day? Did you really have a bad day, or did someone just disagree with you? How quickly anger can turn things into something they're not. As Marcus Aurelius said, "This does not have to turn into anything more than what it is. This does not have to upset you" (*Meditations* 6.52).

If we're mindful of anger when it arises, those moments of mindfulness act as damage control against disruptions in our personal flourishing. We can choose not to let it get us down or hold us back from the person we wish to be. For people who get really angry really fast, it can be hard to catch it and people can say or do things they might not normally do. One strategy is to try and catch it early. It's a lot easier to disengage and cool down when you're irritated than when you're seething with rage. If you can learn to notice what the first signs are that you're getting angry, then you can learn to coach yourself to take a tactical pause to cool down and act with temperance. For many of us, anger tends to build, so a first step toward fostering temperance is mapping out how and where you experience anger in your body.

Take a minute and think about when you get angry. Where do you feel it? Where does it start and how does it build? You might ask your close friends or family members what they observe when you get angry—they might even notice it *before you do*.

_____

_____

_____

_____

_____

Common Signs of Anger

Heart rate speeding up

Upset stomach

Trembling

Clenching

Feeling hot

Changes in breathing pattern

Grinding teeth

Fluctuations in vocal intensity

Pace of speech speeds up or slows down

Shifts in body language

Other: _____

_____

_____

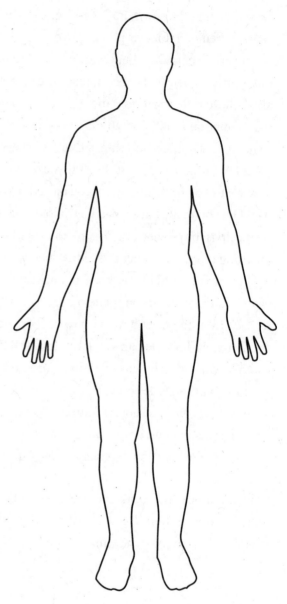

Know Thyself: What Do You Want Your Life to Mean?

As previously mentioned, the Stoics defined wisdom as the knowledge of what's good, which refers to understanding our fundamental life goals. To attain wisdom, it's crucial to know ourselves and be aware of our deepest values and objectives. The process of values clarification, which you did earlier in this chapter, is considered a form of wisdom. Now the final question to ask yourself is: If I were to live a life of fulfillment that was guided by passion and virtue, what would that look like? When Marcus Aurelius wrote the *Meditations*, it was about his life and what Stoicism taught him.

Values Clarification

If I sat down and wrote my own memoir, my version of the classic tome *Meditations*, what would I want it to say?

_____

_____

_____

_____

What kind of life would I need to live to be able to say that?

_____

_____

_____

_____

What would I prioritize in my daily life?

_____

_____

_____

_____

What do I learn about my values from this?

_____

_____

_____

_____

What changes would I need to make?

_____

_____

_____

_____

_____

Adopting a Sage

Now that you've envisioned what you want your life to be about, how do you get there? A Stoic tool that can ease this transformation into who you want to be is the practice of adopting a sage. The ancient Stoics emphasize the importance of striving toward this ideal while acknowledging that true sagehood is extremely rare and challenging, unattainable. However, "adopting a sage" encourages us to continually improve, live in accordance with virtue, and focus on the real goal: the pursuit of wisdom and self-mastery. A wonderful by-product of this pursuit is getting more fulfillment from life by emulating a person we admire; this is motivating and inspires us to trust ourselves as we make decisions with confidence.

Think of someone you admire because they have the courage to live in accordance with values that align with yours. List traits you admire about them and make it a point to embody those. By emulating daily the sage we aspire to be like, we're conditioning ourselves to act in accordance with how we would live and the person we want to be. This may feel strange at first, but remember that emulating isn't faking if you practice this with the intention of carrying these traits throughout the rest of your life.

Who is my sage? _____

What makes them admirable?

_____

_____

_____

What do they believe?

_____

_____

_____

_____

Take a moment to reflect on what you've written. Then, revisit the list daily and strive to adopt one trait each day.

While there are not many things that can be promised in life, despite the initial struggle, we can promise that living in accordance with your values is worth its return on investment. You will grow and unlock new skills and abilities as you become more confident that you're living the life of your choosing. It will leave you feeling self-assured and fulfilled, leading a life that you find personally rewarding. This contributes to lasting inner peace despite the opinions of others or undesirable external circumstances that may befall you.

Chapter 3 Takeaways

- Staying focused on your values and virtues keeps you from spiraling when adversity strikes.

- Happiness can be fleeting, but living in accordance with your values and the Stoic virtues helps you thrive no matter the weather (eudaimonia).

- Values are what's most important to the whole of your life, not just goal-defining moments.

- Wisdom, justice, courage, and temperance lead to greater personal fulfillment and benefit all of society.

- Adopt a sage that has values that align with yours, and work to embody one of their traits each day.

CHAPTER 4

How to Live like a Stoic

Although understanding theory allows us to talk about it, it's the consistent practice that enables us to live it.

—Musonius Rufus, *Lectures* V

Insight is good; insight plus changed behavior is even better. Learning to think like a Stoic is helpful, but how do you actually *live* like a Stoic? It's one thing to decide you want to change, but true change isn't simply a declaration, it's a sustained pattern—similar to how a marriage is much more than a wedding. This chapter will focus on how to create change in your life.

The ancient Stoics would describe your current state as *prokopton* (or *prokoptó*). It means "to progress" and was used to describe the process of making progress toward living a *value-driven* life by examining your actions and thoughts and striving to improve yourself. That's what we, the authors of this book, still strive to do to this day. As Seneca said, "I am here to discuss our shared troubles with you and offer remedies, as though we were both patients in the same hospital" (Letter 27, *On the Shortness of Life*).

So, fellow prokoptons, in this chapter we will take you through simple practices to help you identify and understand your current behaviors and develop a strategy for adopting new behaviors easily. We'll also talk about the last step in your personal development journey, which is how you respond to the world based on your values, something we call Wise Mode. Lastly, we'll be there to support you through the tough moments that often come with the journey toward becoming a flourishing and resilient person. Equipped with a fundamental understanding of what you've read so far about values and virtue, the only person standing between you and the person you would like to be is you. But remember, like the values-driven person you aspire to become, it's all about the journey.

Socrates Challenges the World

As human beings, we all fall into patterns of behavior. Some behaviors are healthy and others are unhealthy, but nevertheless, our daily behavior is a pattern that's shaped by our beliefs, past experiences, worldview, and many other factors. Patterns are easy to adopt but often hard to break. This is because they're very much a part of our identity. You, dear reader and fellow prokopton, picked up this book because you're seeking to become what you want to be: a wiser person who wishes to live a fulfilling, better quality of life. In fact, that's why many of us read books on self-improvement. However, despite reading the texts, many of us also don't benefit. This isn't so much a result of the content of the book as what it requires us to do: challenge our beliefs, behaviors, and, ultimately, ourselves. It's uncomfortable and sometimes even painful.

Socrates made nearly everyone uncomfortable by asking a series of thought-provoking questions, because he aimed to expose contradictions and inconsistencies in their beliefs and actions.

He often led individuals to realize that they didn't truly understand the concepts they claimed to know. And so we must too in order to create lasting change.

In the *Apology*, Plato recounts Socrates's portrayal of Athens as a sizable and lethargic horse, and of Socrates personally as the biting fly that awakens and provokes it. Challenging our comfort zones will sting and leave us itching in discomfort as we let go. But the sting and the itch eventually subside, and the new person you would be forms. Like the biting fly to Athens, these probing inquiries may initially sting and unsettle us, but in time, they lead to a deeper understanding of ourselves, the world around us, and how the person we would be relates to it. Embracing this discomfort is the path to shedding old layers and emerging as the people we aspire to be.

Going Wise Mode

Epictetus wrote, "Every habit and skill is solidified and enhanced through consistent actions, walking through walking, running through running. If you wish to be a good reader, then read; if you wish to be a good writer, then write" (*Discourses* 2.8). To live the life of a Stoic is to become as wise as you can. The sage is a hypothetical ideal and implies this active pursuit. However, the Stoics (as well as logic) tell us that we will never reach an all-knowing state or be the wisest of them all. In fact, like Platonism and Epicureanism, Stoicism was originally called Zenoism, after its founder Zeno. But because the Stoics believed so strongly that this was a common person's philosophy, and that their founders were not infallibly wise, this label was quickly discarded.

The Wise Mode isn't a road to becoming perfect either. However, similar to modes of behavior that keep us stuck, the Wise Mode of behavior aids in propelling us forward by fostering resilience. Wise Mode is the stage at which your consistent practice of Stoic principles and CBT exercises have merged into an instinctive response to situations and events. This paradigm shift is an automatic series of cognitive firings that have become second nature, rather than something one has to actively think about. Right now, you're cultivating not only Stoic philosophy but also CBT practices. Practiced together over time, it evolves into an automatic response that provides the peace of mind that you're making the best possible decisions every day and for your life as a whole.

Figure 2 illustrates the four aspects of Wise Mode. You can find a downloadable copy of the following summary at http://www.newharbinger.com/52663.

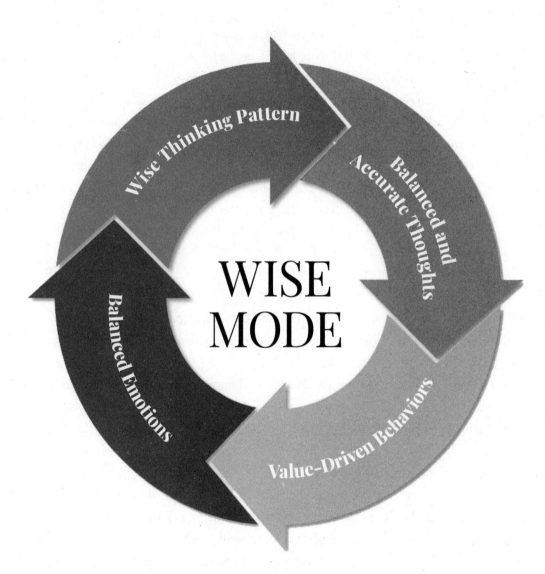

The Four Aspects of Wise Mode

Wise Thinking Patterns

Recognizing and accepting limits of control

Keeping things in perspective

Focus is on how to be effective

Curiosity and empathy

Balanced and Accurate Thoughts

Initial impressions are evaluated

Healthy level of realism in thoughts

Value-Driven Behaviors

Responding instead of reacting

Focusing energies and behaviors on building a meaningful life

Investing energy where change is needed and possible

Letting go of that which doesn't serve you

Balanced Emotions

In touch with emotions, but still in the driver's seat

Tolerating distress in order to live in accordance with values

Full range of emotional experience

Take a moment to flip back to the end of chapter 1 where you set your intentions for using this workbook. Review your intentions and reflect on what you've learned so far. See if there are changes or additions you want to make.

What are my reasons for trying out this workbook?

_____

_____

_____

_____

_____

Do I have specific things I'm hoping to learn?

_____

_____

_____

_____

Do I have specific problems I want to address?

_____

_____

_____

_____

Do I have goals or ambitions I want to work toward?

_____

_____

_____

_____

Are there elements from Wise Mode that I want to add to my list?

_____

_____

_____

If I envision what my life would look like if I were to meet my goals, in as much detail as possible, what would a day in that life look like? In particular, what would other people see me doing if I met my goals? How would an independent observer know, simply by observing, I had met my goals?

_____

_____

_____

_____

_____

Be as specific as possible: What steps can I take *today* to start building this life?

_____

_____

_____

_____

_____

_____

_____

Progress, Not Perfection

Stoic or not, our mind can be a turbulent and unruly realm at times. This is simply a common aspect of the human condition. It's also why the Stoics believe that although we should strive for the sage ideal, we'll never reach it. Philosophy in itself often emphasizes practicality and meaningful action over lofty ideals.

Self-awareness is what the ancient Stoics call *prosoché*. It involves observing our sensations, emotions, and thoughts, directing our focus to the current moment. Put simply, "mindfulness." So, instead of trying to prevent our natural tendencies and initial reactions, we should aim to simply manage them. Instead of expecting perfection, we should practice Stoic mindfulness. The aim is to cultivate the ability to revert to the Stoic practices and CBT exercises contained within this book not as a prevention against mental chaos, but as prevention against being consumed by it.

Stoic Mindfulness

There's Stoic wisdom in the Marcus Aurelius quote, "The path forward lies in overcoming the obstacle. What hinders progress can also serve as the route to success" (*Meditations* 5.20). The hindrance being the route to success is illustrated in how we teach people the skill of mindfulness. Often, an obstacle to being more mindful is a wandering mind (or monkey mind) that seems to erratically jump around. You might say, "I can't learn to deliberately focus on something! My mind is too unfocused." The reality of mindfulness training is that the skill of mindfulness is learning to redirect your attention when it wanders. Repeatedly doing this builds the mental muscle that becomes mindfulness. You can't control whether your mind wanders, but you can control whether you gently bring it back, again and again.

1. Pick anything to focus on (internal or external), such as a spot on the wall, your breath, or a candle flame.

2. Pay attention to that thing.

3. Your mind will automatically wander on its own.

4. Notice that your mind is wandering.

5. Have patience with yourself and gently bring your attention back to what you're focusing on.

6. Repeat steps 3 to 5 often.

Try the reframe that mindfulness is less about your mind never wandering and more about getting really good at bringing your attention back to what you chose to focus on. The skill is really about noticing when your attention wanders and gently bringing it back. From the perspective of cognitive behavioral therapy, mindfulness in itself isn't curative. The idea isn't to practice mindfulness and achieve a Zen state where there are no problems. The idea is that mindfulness can help us mentally decelerate so that we can identify all the choice points that our automatic pilot response is skipping over. Cultivating a practice of mindfulness might be a helpful strategy if you find that you're often given to impulsive behaviors that tend to happen without you even thinking about it.

Think of a time that you did something impulsive. Map out the sequence of events that led up to that impulsive behavior. Try to add as much detail as possible.

_____

_____

_____

_____

_____

_____

_____

_____

_____

Now picture the behavior you would have rather engaged in instead. Envision a revised sequence of events where this time you see yourself doing what you would have rather done instead. Try to add as much detail as possible

_____

_____

_____

_____

_____

Pay attention to the critical junctures where you would have had to implement doing something differently. Notice the distinctive elements of these moments so that you can mentally flag them as times to engage in alternate behaviors in the future. List these critical junctures below.

_____

_____

_____

_____

_____

_____

Mindfulness, like many of the other strategies in this book, is a skill. The more you practice it, the better you will be at it. You need to practice this often to be able to use it well.

How Marcus Aurelius Became Marcus Aurelius

While we consider our own journey of becoming a Stoic, let us see what we can learn from the developmental periods of those who came before us. A number of factors influenced how Marcus Aurelius became the philosopher king that he was. When the heirless Hadrian decided that his nephew's son, the teenage Marcus Aurelius, might have what it took to be emperor, he adopted Antoninus Pius under the condition that Antoninus would in turn adopt Marcus Aurelius, thus giving Marcus a path to succession. Subsequently, he appointed the well-reputed Stoic Junius Rusticus as one of Aurelius's tutors. In his *Meditations* (1.7), Aurelius reflects on what he learned from his mentor:

> Rusticus had a profound impact on me, making me realize the need for self-improvement and discipline. He taught me not to be swayed by vain competition, avoid writing about abstract concepts, refrain from delivering overly persuasive speeches, and not seek recognition for practicing discipline or performing charitable acts. He also advised against indulging in rhetoric, poetry, or extravagant prose.
>
> Additionally, he encouraged me to be quick to forgive those who had offended me through words or actions once they displayed a willingness to reconcile. Rusticus instilled in me the value of reading carefully and not settling for a superficial understanding of a book. Lastly, he introduced me to the teachings of Epictetus from his own collection, for which I am grateful.

The message we can take from Rusticus is that *Stoicism isn't for the fans of a few good quotes, it's a lived philosophy.* Aurelius learned not to focus on artful language and performative gestures to cosplay as a Stoic, but instead to live simply, read carefully, possess humility, and think twice. Also, to live a life guided by wisdom, courage, justice, and temperance. If you desire to get real value out of Stoicism, and to create real lasting change in your life, it must be approached with sincerity and a desire to embrace authenticity and meaningful self-improvement. It's a fundamental truth that change takes practice, and something we can apply to our own lives.

What Epictetus Learned from Musonius

Similarly, what can we learn from the education of Epictetus? One of the most influential Roman Stoics, Gaius Musonius Rufus, was the mentor of the profoundly influential Epictetus, who wrote the *Discourses* or "The Manual" as we know it in modern times. Musonius was well known for his integrity and wisdom, and was a prominent member of the Stoic Opposition to the tyrant Emperor Nero. After returning from his third time being exiled for his opposition, he took Epictetus on as a student. Both men had a profound depth to their philosophy, and it's thought that their adversities of being exiled and enslaved produced a greater capacity for empathy and understanding. They also believed that putting theory into practice holds great significance because it leads to action. Although Musonius's works are limited, it's clear they both employed a straightforward and succinct teaching approach. "Remain mostly quiet, and if you do talk, share only essential words and keep it brief," Epictetus wrote in *Enchiridion* 33. Perhaps this is why the *Enchiridion* is often described as no-nonsense in its delivery.

As we embark on the path to becoming Stoics, it's worth considering what insights Epictetus gained from Musonius regarding this very journey, which could guide us in emulating their example. Epictetus says, "The philosopher's classroom serves as a 'clinic': when you leave, you shouldn't feel elation but rather a certain unease, similar to how you don't enter in perfect condition in the first place" (*Discourses*, III.24.20).

Today, we use the word "therapeutic" to mean something is soothing or that something involves the painful work of addressing the underlying issues. A dentist might use a local anesthetic to dull the pain of a procedure, which helps, though the main value of the process is addressing the underlying problem. Stoicism isn't meant to be Novocain but the drill. Similar to the practice of physical therapy where we focus on diligently doing difficult (and sometimes painful) tasks to increase our flexibility and functionality, to Epictetus, Stoicism isn't meant to make us avoid pain but rather to confront and work through it. On the other side of this short-lived discomfort is the lifelong reward of living well. As Musonius Rufus wrote, "When you achieve something worthwhile through hard work, the effort quickly fades, but the positive result lasts. On the other hand, if you do something disgraceful for the sake of instant gratification, the pleasure vanishes rapidly, while the shame persists" (*Fragments* 51). We can learn something from Epictetus's journey to apply to our own lives.

Overcoming Obstacles on the Prokopton's Journey

The prokopton's journey is one of progressing toward wisdom and balance. However, Stoicism doesn't make us exempt from feeling resistance from our environment or experiencing moments of self-doubt. Would we expect it to be easy to swim against a current that's been flowing in the same direction for years, maybe decades? Of course not. When we change, our environment responds. Just as Aurelius prepared himself each morning to encounter resistant people by expecting them, so too should we expect to encounter people in our lives who won't entirely understand our pursuits. It's important to be mindful as well when we're taking on too much at once. A good indicator of this is overwhelming feelings of self-doubt that have our minds running back to its worn patterns, the agreeable behavior that's familiar but that ultimately holds us back. These are simply the growing pains that accompany change. By embracing these challenges rather than sacrificing our authenticity for approval or to avoid vulnerability, we will gain something much greater: a fulfilling life that retains meaning no matter what happens.

It's useful to bear in mind that the *Meditations* of Marcus Aurelius are not necessarily his teachings. They are collective notes on what Stoicism taught him and its proven effectiveness in nearly every aspect of his life. The learning never stopped, for this Roman emperor remained a true student until his death. As we've mentioned, he placed a lot of emphasis on impermanence but also change. Marcus Aurelius believed that change is an inherent and fundamental aspect of the universe, echoing the philosophy of the pre-Socratic thinker Heraclitus. As Socrates expressed in Plato's *Cratylus*, Heraclitus's insight that "Change is the only constant in life" remains a timeless and profound idea. Marcus Aurelius also recognized that with change often comes a loss or letting go of something that we may have become attached to, such as comfort zones or the need to be accepted. For although death is a fate we all share, living in stagnation and relying on external circumstances to make us happy is a waking death; the goal of Stoicism is to focus on flourishing and living a full life guided by what matters most.

Chapter 4 Takeaways

- Change is a process.

- Old patterns can feel automatic due to a variety of factors.

- A Wise Mode of being includes wise patterns of thinking, balanced and accurate thoughts, value-driven behaviors, and balanced emotions.

- You can use your Stoic skills to help foster a pattern of Stoic living.

CHAPTER 5

From Demandingness to Acceptance

Circumstances do not bend to our expectations. Events unfold in their own way, and people act as they will. By abiding by this, life will be tranquil.

—Epictetus, *Enchiridion* 8

Gaius Musonius Rufus was one of the major Roman Stoic philosophers in the first century. His wisdom and integrity earned him such profound respect that contemporary scholars occasionally liken him to the "Socrates of Rome." Musonius was among the Stoics who opposed the tyrant Emperor Nero as well. In the face of exile, due to their opposition, one of Musonius's allies, Thrasea, expressed they would rather be killed than face banishment. Musonius didn't share this conclusion, however. "If you decide on death as the greater evil," he began, "what rationale underlies that? Or, if you decide to accept it as the lesser of two evils, don't forget the one who offered you this choice. Why not attempt to embrace what has been bestowed upon you?" (Epictetus, *Discourses* 1.1.26). The focus of this chapter is the idea of reconciling with reality while maintaining resilience and perseverance. Its wisdom helps us recognize that what has happened has already happened, and helps us focus our efforts on what we actually have control over—ourselves. We will revisit the wisdom and insights of Musonius in a later chapter.

Also consider the example of the philosopher Epictetus. He was enslaved from birth and there are accounts of him having lameness in one of his legs due to the harsh physical abuse he experienced at the hands of his slavers. And yet despite this, he wrote, "Sickness obstructs the body, but not the will, unless it so desires. Lameness hinders the leg, but not the will. Keep this in mind for every eventuality. You'll notice it might hinder something else, but not your core self" (*Enchiridion* 9). He also wrote, "You can shackle my leg, but even Zeus can't overcome my freedom of will" (*Discourses* 1.1). Meaning you can chain my leg, but you can't chain my mind. From this we learn that while we can't always control our circumstances, we can control how we choose to respond to those circumstances, even when they're painful and unjust. To explore how we might respond to distressing situations, let's look at the examples of Linda and Leon in the following stories.

Linda is very active in her faith but her adult children are not. She's expressed many times that she wants them to attend church, but the more she brings it up, the less they want to talk about it.

What do you suppose would happen if she were to try even harder? Maybe she could try forcing them to listen to her read the scriptures. Perhaps she could mail them her church's sermon schedule. Or, if she could ask evangelists to visit them, maybe they could get through to them. Although, she could try and trick them into coming over for dinner while the minister is there.

Will these escalations help her get what she wants? Is it possible that it would backfire and her children would become even more distant?

What are Linda's expectations?

_____

_____

Are her expectations within her control?

_____

How does her attempt to control the situation affect things?

_____

Leon is running late for an appointment, driving on the freeway in the passing lane. The driver in front of him isn't going fast enough for his liking. The left lane is meant for passing! he thinks to himself. A rage builds inside his chest as he screams at the car in front of him, "Would it kill ya to speed up, guy?! I'm gonna be late because of you!"

Will intensifying his behaviors move the car out of the way? Perhaps he could try incessantly honking and shaking his fist. If he tailgates the car, the driver might pick up the pace. He could take the risk and pass the driver on the shoulder.

Will any of these options get Leon what he wants? It's possible the car could move out of the way for his unhinged behavior. But his attitude could make the driver resent this unruly response, and then slow down out of spite. The odds of the worst-case scenario is becoming more and more likely the more Leon engages in this aggressive behavior: getting pulled over by the police or causing an accident, possibly even killing someone in the process. This would have been a far more detrimental and lasting consequence than simply being late.

What are Leon's expectations?

_____

_____

Are his expectations within his control?

_____

How does his attempt to control the situation affect things?

_____

It's All Uphill from Here: Sisyphus's Eternity

According to Greek mythology, Sisyphus was famously punished by Hades, who forced him to spend every day rolling a huge boulder up a hill for all eternity. He was never able to accomplish his task. The problem wasn't that he didn't try hard enough, it was that he was trying to do the *impossible*. The story served in ancient times to describe what Hell is actually like.

Humans fall into patterns of creating a life like Sisyphus's punishment when they put all their time and energy into trying to do something that they know deep down is unachievable. Fighting against reality can be a hell unto itself. As Marsha Linehan, the founder of dialectical behavior therapy (DBT), said, "Acceptance is the only way out of hell" (Linehan 2014, 461). Now Sisyphus was doomed to an eternity of this, but we as humans have the ability to recognize patterns and make changes.

Where do I see other people stuck in a pattern such as the one Sisyphus was in?

_____

_____

_____

How does this endless pursuit affect them?

_____

_____

_____

If they were to disengage from this pattern, where could they spend their time and energy instead?

_____

_____

_____

What kind of life would I want for them?

_____

_____

_____

If I were in their position, what would I want to do?

_____

_____

_____

Living in Agreement with Nature

Marcus Aurelius encapsulates what it means to live in accordance with nature in _Meditations_ 2.17:

> Human life is fleeting, our bodies are in constant change, our perceptions are limited, our physical composition is subject to decay, our thoughts are ever-shifting, luck is unpredictable, and fame lacks judgment. In essence, our physical existence flows like a river, our mental state is akin to a dream or vapor, life is a battle in unfamiliar territory, and posthumous recognition fades into obscurity. So, what guides us? Philosophy alone. Philosophy means maintaining inner harmony, resisting external pressures, enduring pain and pleasure with purpose, acting sincerely, not relying on others, embracing life's events and circumstances as part of our journey, and facing death with serenity as it's merely the dissolution of our elemental makeup. If the natural world undergoes constant change without harm, why fear the transformation and dissolution of our own elements? It's all in accordance with nature, and nothing natural can be considered evil.

Stoicism holds that there's a rational order to the universe, which is often referred to as "Nature" or "the Logos." To live in agreement with nature, the Stoics believe that we should align our thoughts, actions, and desires with this rational order. This involves recognizing and accepting the natural course of events, including our own mortality, rather than resisting or being upset by them. We can respond with resilience instead of fear.

Living in harmony with nature entails aligning our lives with reason, employing our rational faculties to steer our actions and choices. Although we may be a lot like animals, the chief trait that separates us is this ability to reason. So, while a dog may naturally bark or bite when it feels threatened, we can't (or *shouldn't*) do this to our boss or spouse. Such behavior goes against human reasoning, which *is* natural for us. We have the capacity to pause and calculate the risks without indulging in our excessive emotions; we can suspend judgment and examine our initial impressions. We can behave as Marcus Aurelius wrote: "If external factors cause you distress, the suffering doesn't arise from the thing itself but rather from your assessment of it; and this assessment is within your power to alter at any time" (*Meditations* 8.47). Similarly, the Serenity Prayer is a mantra for nearly every 12-step recovery program: "God, grant me the serenity to accept the things I cannot change, the courage to change the things I can, and the wisdom to know the difference."

Fighting against the things we can't change is what causes the most discord in our lives. If we choose not to accept the reality of a situation, it doesn't change the situation but only makes how we feel about it worse. It causes emotional disruption, which is what prompts us to seek anything to numb it instead of actively working out how we feel. But so often we choose vice over coping because it's seemingly easier in the moment. It doesn't make *life* easier, though. Reality is there waiting when we sober up, and the more we deny it, the more vice we seek. If we embrace reality and the adversity that may come with it, we maintain the direction of our lives. As philosopher Bion of Borysthenes illustrates, "Should you try to pick up a snake at the center of its body, you will surely be bitten. If you take hold of it at the head, however, it's unable to bite you" (Teles of Megara, *On Self-Sufficiency*). Embrace the uncomfortable and the uncomfortable loses its power over you. Living in agreement with nature is also the basis of acceptance and commitment therapy (ACT) and cognitive behavioral therapy (CBT), which encourage people to embrace their feelings as opposed to living in denial or shame of them.

Amor Fati

Amor fati, a Latin phrase commonly used in Stoicism, means "love of one's fate," or in a modern context "embracing one's fate." Embracing our fate isn't a passive attitude but rather a proactive one. Instead of resisting fate, embracing it provides more information as we work with it and not against it. The wisdom of this mantra pairs well with the wisdom from an old song by Crosby, Stills, and Nash, who sing about a situation where we might not be with the person we want to be with, but we can love the person we're with. While our fate might not be the life we would have chosen, this is the life that we have, and when it's over there might not be any do-overs. So, what do we do? Do we live a life of bitter resentment that this isn't what we wanted? Or do we embrace our fate and try to make the most of it?

Stoic philosophers Chrysippus and Zeno agreed on an analogy that birthed one of the most famous proverbs on acceptance: "A dog tied to the cart must follow it for it has no choice, even if it doesn't know where it's headed or why it's headed there. Although the dog may struggle against moving in that direction and attempt to pull away, the dog is ultimately powerless to the direction of the cart" (Hippolytus, *Refutation of All Heresies* 1.21). The moral of the story? "Let go or be dragged."

In the same way, we're bound to the course of fate and must accept what happens to us, even when we don't like or understand it. This allows us to focus on what's in our control. What we do next will determine our future. If *amor fati* means loving your fate, then it's necessary to take a long-term perspective. The next time we feel as if despair is about to swallow us because of unfortunate circumstances, we can remind ourselves of *amor fati*; our acceptance isn't a final destination, but rather grants permission for a new beginning. An attitude of acceptance takes power from events and gives it back to us, helping us find meaning and purpose in difficult situations. In other words, it's another means of knowing ourselves.

Radical Acceptance

One of the core teachings of dialectical behavior therapy is the concept of radical acceptance. When we encounter a situation that seems intolerable or unacceptable, our emotional response might be to lash out in anger or to avoid the situation and feel hopeless. Radical acceptance is a distress tolerance skill. The idea is to hold the situation in such a way that what we do in the short term doesn't make things worse in the long term. This often means viscerally forcing our mind to accept reality as it is. It doesn't necessarily always have to be this way, but we must first accept what has happened if we're ever to move beyond it. This deep level of deliberate acceptance is called radical acceptance.

In economics the term "opportunity cost" means that if we say yes to one thing, we say no to something else. Therefore, every choice we make has a cost of a lost opportunity. Time spent in nonacceptance has the opportunity cost of the time and energy you could have spent doing something you actually care about. As Seneca said, "While we wait for life, life passes" (*On Saving Time*, Letters 1.1).

How much of my time and energy goes into nonacceptance?

_____

_____

What opportunities have I missed out on because I couldn't let go?

_____

_____

Where would I rather invest that time and energy?

_____

_____

Reality doesn't wait for us to accept it in order to exist. Acceptance simply means that we're operating on the principle of reality, not fighting against it. Military culture has a mantra of "embrace the suck." The notion is that sometimes things are unpleasant but unavoidable, especially if progress is to be made. In these situations, sometimes the wisest thing you can do is embrace the situation as reality and try to make the most of it.

We can strongly dislike a situation and still accept that things are as they are. Imagine if we go to pull a door and it won't open. Once we look up, we notice there's a sign on the door in bold letters that says "push." Radical acceptance is recognizing that what we're trying to do isn't going to work. Instead of trying to force the door open by pulling it, and possibly breaking the doorframe, we can push the door open and take the action that's available to us. This might be a simple example, but in real life, acceptance is often most needed in difficult situations.

If we're drowning in a white water rapid and don't know how to swim, the fundamental solution is to learn to swim. However, at this moment it wouldn't be effective for someone to stand on the bank of the river and describe how to do the breaststroke. What we'd need right now is a flotation device. And, importantly, our goal is to get through the situation without making it worse. Swallowing water may be unavoidable, but the goal is to minimize the amount and survive. When we get to a calmer part of the river, our goals can change from there. Calmer water would be a more ideal place to learn to swim. If you've ever been on a river, you know there's a constant transition from rapid, to calm, to rapid, and back to calm. Our goals should change with the river. Radical acceptance is often a good approach to getting through life circumstances without making a situation worse.

The human brain evolved to be really good at problem solving, maybe a little too good. As famed psychologist Abraham Maslow said, "If the only tool you have is a hammer, you tend to see every problem as a nail" (Maslow 1966, 15–16). The brain is so good at solving problems that it can see every situation as a problem to be solved, even if we ourselves can't solve it. Thus, the brain tends to drift into problem-solving mode in the face of what it views as a potential problem. So, radically accepting a situation isn't a onetime event. We can accept something and come to terms with it, refocusing our efforts on what's in the realm of our control, and our mind will probably drift back to that default place of nonacceptance. Therefore, we must turn the mind (and heart) toward acceptance over and over. How do we do this?

A useful technique for facilitating radical acceptance is to recite certain Stoic sayings. For example, when confronting something upsetting that you can't control, try to let go of the struggle with the uncontrollable by saying, "Whatever things we cannot control. Tell me the upshot. They are nothing to me" (Epictetus, *Discourses* 3.16). How you say this in your mind (or aloud) matters. It will take some personal experimentation to understand the differential impact of various approaches to recitation, as words have a limited ability to convey important nuances.

Accepting What Is Hard to Accept

One of the more difficult parts about the skill of radical acceptance is that the places where we need it the most are often the ones that are the hardest and most painful to accept. One strategy is to try incorporating the principles of dialectical behavior therapy. Dialectics means seeking a more nuanced view of a situation by attending to and synthesizing truths from both sides of a paradox. For example, we might be in a position where we need to do better than we are, but we're doing the best we can. This creates a state of tension and paradox. We can try to resolve this paradox by holding on to both pieces at once, saying, "I am doing the best I can and I need to do better." Of course, by continuing to do the best we can, our best will only get better. Freedom to improve the situation is found by accepting the reality of what's happening.

As Tara Brach, the author of *Radical Acceptance*, wrote, "The boundary to what we can accept is the boundary to our freedom" (Brach 2004, 44).

Psychologist Hank Robb suggests a strategy where people sort the problems they're dealing with by whether it's your fault that it happened and whether it's your responsibility to address. A common challenge is the situation where something isn't our fault but is still our responsibility to deal with. The very painful truth is that the situation we're in might be completely unfair. We might be suffering for something that we didn't choose or cause, and often no one is coming to rescue us. Radical acceptance is stopping to ask yourself, "What are my options?" and "What am I going to do?" and then taking action.

Sort some of your problems into categories of whether they're the result of your actions, and whether they're your responsibility to address. The aim is not to assign blame, but rather to see what to focus on and what to let go of.

Not My Fault & Not My Responsibility to Solve	Not My Fault & My Responsibility to Solve
My Fault & Not My Responsibility to Solve	My Fault & My Responsibility to Solve

Where do I need to focus my efforts?

_____

_____

_____

_____

What do I need to let go of?

_____

_____

_____

_____

Another option for acceptance is to hold on to both sides of the dilemma at the same time. We can self-validate why it makes sense that we're upset *and at the same time* focus on the need for acceptance. For example, it might be true to say:

This situation isn't my fault *and* it's still my responsibility to solve the problem.

It's unfair that this happened *and* this is what happened.

I completely hate this situation *and* it is what it is.

None of this would have happened if people had done what they were supposed to do *and* I have to play the cards that I was dealt.

I'm really worried about how this is going to turn out *and* I did everything I can; now it's out of my hands.

Try putting together a statement where you join both the reason that it's hard to accept it and the reality that you have to accept it. Using the word "and" between both statements is a way to honor both sides. You can find a downloadable copy of this exercise at http://www.newharbinger.com/52663.

Both Are True		
Why This Is Hard to Accept	AND	The Reality That I Have to Accept It
Example: What they did was wrong.	and	I can't change what happened.

While practicing the skill of acceptance, be wary of the pitfall of resignation. The goal isn't to live a life of indifference, but rather to radically accept what you can't change in order to weather the storms of life and not make things worse. Focus your energies and efforts on building a life that's full of meaning and guided by your values. You'll have a lot more time and energy to invest in building a life worth living if you can let go of and accept the things you can't control.

Chapter 5 Takeaways

- When your expectations rise to the level of demands, you may exacerbate your distress, be less effective at solving problems, and be distracted from living vitally.

- Demands involve insisting that the world be different than it is.

- *Amor fati*, embracing fate, involves recognizing there's a flow to life, and thriving means focusing on what comes next.

- Radical acceptance is a core strategy for contending with things beyond your control.

- Acceptance isn't resignation.

CHAPTER 6

Tolerating Discomfort and Decreasing Suffering

Our suffering is created more in our mind and exists less in reality.

—Seneca, *On Groundless Fear* 13.4

The easiest and most effective way to avoid stressful situations is to simply avoid them. The easiest and most effective way to overcome anxiety, however, is by subjecting yourself to those same stressful situations. When we trade in emotional discomfort for the brief freedom from having to feel it, we're no longer in control of our own lives and have let fear essentially make decisions for us.

The best of intentions will never be a foolproof line of defense against stressful or even tragic events befalling us. When the unfortunate does occur, we're presented with an immediate choice: endure the long-lasting effects on our well-being, or cope healthily by using our wisdom to see the grand scheme.

Cato the Younger: Stress Exposure and Doing the Right Thing

In Plato's *Republic*, Socrates asserts that the truly wise individual understands that excessive complaining when faced with misfortunes yields no benefit, as "there is no advantage in taking them to heart."

Drawing upon similar principles of self-discipline and resilience, Cato the Younger, a Roman statesman and orator who was greatly influenced by the teachings of Cleanthes, lived simply, valued integrity, and put his life on the line in opposition to the rise of Julius Caesar and his dictatorship. Famously, he also willingly exposed himself to stress in the name of self-discipline and the pursuit of virtue. Plutarch, a biographer and Platonist of the time, records that Cato would engage in wearing a heavy helmet and even heavier armor during his daily activities to build endurance and resilience against pain. He would also perform long marches and drills on his own accord wearing this hot, cumbersome gear to strengthen his mind as well as his body.

Now, it wasn't the reputation he was aiming for in his voluntary stress exercises. It was to adopt and foster the perspective that there's reward that lies beyond the endurance of stress. Although he proved this many times in his career, this perspective was never more evident than when he was urged to seek an oracle to predict the outcome of his upcoming battle against Caesar. He dismissed this idea because to him, that wasn't the point. Even if it was prophesied that he would lose, he was not going to retreat because rising up against tyranny is simply the right thing to do.

Cato's enduring legacy isn't solely based on his military and political trajectory but rather his unwavering commitment to his principles and integrity. It's this steadfast resolve, refusing to yield to suffering, that he's remembered for most today. His life and actions resonated deeply with later Stoic philosophers, such as Seneca, Epictetus, and Marcus Aurelius. Often cited as an exemplar of Stoic virtues, Cato used his actions to illustrate the Stoic concept of living in accordance with nature and reason. His moral integrity, self-control, and willingness to confront challenges aligned with Stoic teachings about the importance of cultivating virtue and responding to adversity with wisdom.

In the end, the armies of Caesar defeated the armies of the Senate. The new emperor offered to pardon those who had stood in opposition to him, if they recognized his authority. Cato's commitment to Stoic principles and his unwavering adherence to his values dictated that he could not collude with this injustice. So instead of legitimizing the dictatorship rule of Julius Caesar, he chose death over tyranny. His integrity made him a prominent figure in the Stoic tradition. His actions and character served as an inspiration for later Stoic philosophers and continue to be referenced as a powerful example of Stoic ethics and virtue.

The hand of fate is over us, and Heav'n

Exacts severity from all our thoughts.

It's not now a time to talk of aught

But chains or conquest, liberty or death.

—Joseph Addison, *Cato, a Tragedy* (1713), Act II, Scene 4

Before the American Revolution, there existed a theatrical production known as *Cato, A Tragedy*. This play depicted the final moments of Cato the Younger. This narrative of fighting against tyrants was well received at the time, and Cato became a role model for George Washington, who had a performance of the play performed at Valley Forge during the war. Several important quotes from the American Revolution were supposedly derived from this play, including Patrick Henry's "Give me liberty, or give me death," and Nathan Hale's "I regret that I have but one life to lose for my country" (see Harper 2014). The courage and integrity of Cato would echo through the ages.

So, why should we be more like Cato and make doing the right thing our top priority no matter how painful? Because beyond the veil of fear and discomfort that often accompanies doing what's right lies liberation from being bound by the whims of fate and external circumstances dictated by the world. Hopefully, just as the highly regarded Stoics, others will follow our example. This chapter focuses on how to increase your ability to tolerate discomfort so you can focus on living well in the long term.

Musonius Rufus and the Importance of Experiential Practice

Gaius Musonius Rufus, one of the four great Roman Stoics, emphasized the importance of behavioral practice in learning to live stoically. This contrasts with trying to learn Stoicism through purely, or mostly, intellectual means. He offered several analogies to support his point, including the differential skill realized by a musician learning to play their instrument through book study rather than many hours of playing. This practice of training both the mind and the body has direct implications for distress tolerance. A core idea of Stoicism is that in adversity lies the opportunity for growth. If we can train ourselves to deliberately do things that are difficult (but not actually dangerous), we can build our distress tolerance muscles.

Consider the example of swimming in cold water. Although it isn't recorded that the ancient Stoics practiced cold water exposure, ice baths, and cold showers, many modern-day Stoics take up this practice to build mental endurance. While it isn't a necessary component of the philosophy, it's worth mentioning that exposure to cold stimulates the body's natural response to stress, which leads to the release of hormones such as adrenaline, noradrenaline, and endorphins. The same happens when we initially take a dip in the pool or the ocean. It's quite a shock at first, but the more we bathe in the icy cold water, the more we adapt. The same is said for stressful situations. They'll arise, but if we're willing to stay and wade, the initial jarring feeling wears off, enabling us to swim instead of run out.

In modern military culture, there's a saying, "train like you fight, and fight like you train." If we want to be able to tolerate the distress that comes from the realities of life, Stoic wisdom would suggest we need to practice exposing ourselves to such stress.

Building Distress Tolerance

Tolerating discomfort is best learned through repeated practice involving willing exposure to discomfort. In this practice, mindset is key. If we approach this as an opportunity for training and strength building, it will be more effective than if we view it as an unendurable hardship. The more variable the discomfort type, the more expansive the learning. It can be useful to organize your practice categorically, involving the physical, emotional, and cognitive domains. It's also helpful to identify practices that can become part of your daily or weekly routine. Consider adopting some of the discomfort tolerance exercises listed below.

Physical

- Take a cold shower.

- Periodically give up a preferred food, or drink black coffee instead of sweetened.

- Commit to taking the stairs in lieu of elevators.

- Park a few blocks away from your destination so that you have to walk.

- Perform planks and other forms of exercise.

- Hold a piece of ice in your hand.

Emotional

- Watch a movie that elicits an uncomfortable emotion.

- Read an uncomfortable news story.

- Have an important but uncomfortable conversation.

- Stop what you're doing and momentarily sit with whatever emotion you're currently experiencing.

- Recall something you really want but you can never have and sit with it for a defined period of time.

Cognitive

- Engage in a cognitively strenuous activity that you dislike (such as a difficult puzzle).

- Learn something in a subject that doesn't come easily for you.

- Recall a memory that makes you feel angry or sad. Then strive to view it through a lens of indifference with phrases like "I can't change the past and so I won't let it affect my present and future" or "Let it be what it is, and not an anchor to my development."

- Identify things in your life that perhaps you've long been unsatisfied with. Instead of being overwhelmed by them, view these undesired occurrences one at a time and analyze them objectively. Offer yourself the same advice you would give a good friend about how to approach these situations.

These are only examples. Can you identify additional practices? If so, list them here:

_____

_____

_____

_____

_____

_____

_____

Once you've identified one or more exercises, specify how frequently you will practice. For example:

- Take a cold shower once a week.

- Give up a preferred food for a month.

- Randomly select one practice exercise to engage in weekly.

The View from Above

So many of us are white-knuckling it through life without realizing it. Much like the horrors of uncertainty, a lot of our woes about a situation stem from its effect on our imagination. We have the power, however, to obtain all of the clarity we can about a situation, making us surer of ourselves, if we take on a "view from above" perspective.

The "view from above" is a Stoic visualization technique to help us get some distance from the situation (otherwise known as "cognitive distancing") in order to see all facets of it. One of the many ancient inspirations for this technique is the mythology of the gods residing on Mt. Olympus. From that vantage, they could see over all of humankind. From high above, metaphorically speaking, we can see everything in the grand scheme and, in turn, gain a "higher perspective." This is a perspective that's detached and objective, allowing us to gain a more comprehensive and unbiased understanding of a situation. Biases can be dangerous because they can lead to unfair or inaccurate judgments when we make decisions. We often take these mental shortcuts or make assumptions based on our own experiences and beliefs, thus influencing how we perceive and interpret information. Biases prevent us from considering all the available evidence and can lead us to make decisions that are not in our own best interests or the best interests of others. The best, just, and most confidently made decisions are informed ones, and this is precisely what the view from above can grant.

For example, you've been dumped by both your significant other and your employer...*at the same time!* Boom. Rock bottom. With a bruised ego (and butt), how do you expect to recover? First of all, we can't see from all the way down here. You see that small spool of rope, the one that's about the width of your ankle? Yeah. Step into that if you would, please. We hope you're not afraid of heights...

YOINK!

Whoa! Look at you go! I'll bet you can see all kinds of things from up there, suspended far above this pit of feelings. What's that? You can see the opportunity to reinvent yourself? A clean slate so you don't have to say, "If I could do it all over again..." because that's quite literally what you have the chance to do now? There's *freedom* in that, you say? My partner's mom was a pain in the *what* anyway?!

And there you have it, the view from above. No, it isn't all the blood that just rushed to your head that's giving you that light feeling. You chose your perspective well, the perspective of a wise person. While we won't be there to set booby traps, the next time you're feeling helpless in a situation, you can climb into a cognitive gondola basket and sail that brain-balloon high above the external stimuli of the world below!

You can draw your own version of figure 3 with a pencil and paper to help obtain the view from above when you feel helpless. In the speck that is you lies your feelings about the situation, initial impressions and assumptions, and so on. In the large circle, outside of you, are other people in the situation, factors you may have not yet considered, possible solutions, and other elements only seen in the grand scheme of things.

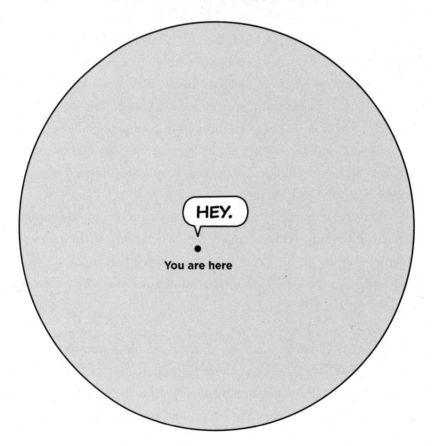

Let's use the example of an individual who is concerned about the impacts of climate change on their community, namely the carbon dioxide emissions that using mass amounts of energy can cause. They may initially feel disheartened by the scale of the problem. When faced with issues such as pollution, deforestation, or climate change, it can be easy to feel overwhelmed and power-less. However, by taking a step back and considering the larger context in which these issues are occurring, it may be possible to see that these challenges are also opportunities to create a more sustainable and equitable future (see figure 4).

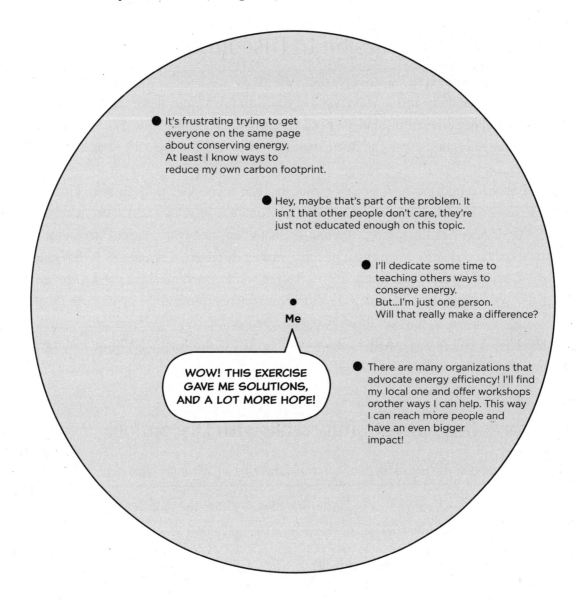

Remember that Stoicism was born from a reversal of fortune. We must remember too, though, that the reversal of fortune was first a choice in perspective. Had Zeno given up after he lost everything, he wouldn't have found the wisdom of Socrates that inspired his empowering school of thought that has been so useful, to so many, for centuries. You can flip the script; it's in your power to do so. If you can pause and take inventory of the grand scheme, you will go from powerless to powered up. This is how you can begin to take control of your destiny, your life.

Exploring Our Aversion to Discomfort

The previous example is one way to apply the "view from above": seeing the opportunity in a bad situation. However, there are numerous ways in which the view from above can benefit your life and mental wellness when applied in daily life. For example, it can help you gain useful distance from troubling thoughts, so you can disentangle from them and see them for what they are: just thoughts.

The Stoics considered how troubling thoughts add more pain to a distressing situation. Seneca wrote, "How does lamenting problems contribute to making them seem more significant?" (*Moral Letters* 78.13). Indeed, pain and discomfort are an intrinsic part of life; a wise Stoic doesn't focus on trying to avoid this. The Stoic view of dispreferred sensations is that fighting against them only makes them worse. For example, if you feel emotional pain and then become upset that you are unhappy, you now have both the emotional pain and the upset about the pain. So how do we tolerate feelings of distress? Consider the following exercise developed by psychologist Hank Robb (2022). You can find a downloadable copy of this exercise at http://www.newhar binger.com/52663.

══════ Becoming Comfortable with Discomfort ══════

Identify an emotion you're feeling that you would describe as discomfortable: _____

On a scale of 1 to 100, where 1 = no distress at all and 100 = the most intense distress you've ever felt, rate your discomfort: _____

Next, divide this number into two components:

- the literal, actual sensations you feel

- the "I don't want these sensations!" reaction that you have toward the literal, actual sensations

Which piece is bigger? _____

If the "I don't want these sensations!" reaction that you have toward the literal, actual sensations was bigger, divide that into its components:

- "I just don't want these sensations."

- "I MUST NOT have these sensations."

Which piece is bigger? _____

Try focusing on your discomfort while telling yourself how miserable it is. What happens when you tell yourself that it's unbearable or that you can't stand it?

_____

_____

_____

Try focusing on your discomfort while telling yourself how bearable it is. What happens when you tell yourself that though it's unpleasant you can bear it?

_____

_____

_____

What did you learn from this?

_____

_____

_____

_____

Cognitive behavioral therapists have identified two similar cognitive patterns that tend to exacerbate unnecessary suffering: catastrophizing and awfulizing. Catastrophizing means predicting catastrophic outcomes and awfulizing means viewing things as worse than they are.

Activating Event: What happened?

_____

_____

_____

Belief: What thoughts, worries, images, or predictions were going through my head?

_____

_____

_____

Consequence: How did that make me feel? What did that make me do?

_____

_____

_____

Sometimes our anxious thoughts try to trick us into believing them using something called "catastrophizing." This includes overpredicting the likelihood something bad will happen and underpredicting our ability to cope with it.

Describe an upcoming event that you are anxious about.

_____

_____

_____

What's the *worst-case* scenario?

_____

_____

_____

What's the *best-case* scenario?

_____

_____

_____

What's the *most likely* scenario?

_____

_____

_____

Sometimes we have irrational beliefs such as "awfulizing." These create unnecessary suffering by causing us to believe that things are worse than they actually are. This often leads to ineffective behavioral responses.

If my prediction happened, would it truly be awful/terrible/unbearable?

_____

_____

Can I try telling myself that it might be bad, but not terrible or unbearable?

_____

_____

What's my new perspective?

_____

_____

_____

How does this make me feel and what does this make me want to do?

_____

_____

Is this in line with my long-term goals and values?

_____

_____

After the event happens, answer these questions:

What actually happened?

_____

_____

_____

What did I learn?

_____

_____

_____

Premeditatio Malorum

Donald Robertson (2019) said in his best-selling book *How to Think Like a Roman Emperor* that Stoicism is going from *what if?* to *so what?* Premeditatio Malorum (or cognitive rehearsal) is mentally rehearsing the anticipated event and visualizing the worst-case scenario. So what if the worst happens? It helps to analyze what that means, what that looks like, to see how much it really doesn't matter in the long run. People who give in to anxious worry do an ineffective version of this; they picture what might happen and agonize over how awful or intolerable that would be. A Stoic pictures what could happen and practices sitting with that with Stoic resilience and indifference. Yes, bad things might happen and, no, it won't destroy me. This is an important aspect of the practice. That uncomfortability doesn't last long and you're more likely to be inoculated to the feeling if you keep rehearsing that moment over and over. It's like time travel: you'll already have *been there, done that* so much that it lessens the emotional impact. As Seneca said, "The more you anticipate it, the less upsetting it will be when it arrives" (*On the Healing Power of the Mind*, Letter 78).

Premeditatio Malorum has been deemed by some as "negative visualization," but it isn't as pessimistic as it sounds. It's actually taking the negative and desaturating it of its negative effect. Premeditatio Malorum helps us claim victory over any limits that the emotional effect of adversity has. It gives us the courage to make decisions and do what's in our best interest, all things considered. Like a shadowboxer, the wise person prepares themselves for adversity so that they can be mentally prepared and therefore resilient.

Seneca again makes a strong case for the premeditation of adversity in his letter to Lucilius (76.34–35):

> The foolish and those who rely on luck perceive each new event as an entirely novel and unexpected challenge. For the inexperienced, much of the difficulty they face comes from the novelty of their situation. However, those who are wise habituate themselves to impending hardships by contemplating them over a long period of time, thereby reducing their severity. The wise person recognizes that all things are possible, and they can say with confidence, "I knew it," no matter what circumstances arise.

Seneca's "The things hardest to bear are sweetest to remember" becomes all the truer when we've prepared for the worst only to receive the best or even the not-so-bad. A downloadable copy of this exercise is available at http://www.newharbinger.com/52663.

Changing "What If?" to "So What?"

What is something I need to do but have been putting off because I dread how unpleasant it might be?

_____

Why is it important to do this thing?

_____

_____

_____

When I think about doing this thing, what in my mind is the worst part of it?

_____

_____

_____

Am I more bothered by how bad I think it will be? Or by how poorly I think I'll be able to tolerate it?

_____

_____

If the problem is I'm afraid of how unbearable the situation might be, can I practice viewing it from a perspective of Stoic indifference?

_____

_____

If the problem is I'm doubting my ability to withstand discomfort, can I practice viewing the situation while reminding myself of my own resilience?

_____

_____

What happens when I tell myself this might be uncomfortable but not unbearable?

_____

_____

_____

Memento Mori

> You could die shortly. Let what you do, say, and think be based on that notion.
>
> —Marcus Aurelius, *Meditations* 2.11

If you were given twenty-four hours to live, what would you do with it? Would you spend it with the people you cherish the most? Would you tell your friends, spouse, and children just how much you love them? Would this prompt you to also express what you've been longing to say about injustices? Would you even tell your crush how you felt about them? If tomorrow isn't guaranteed, then why aren't you spending your life like this right now?

Memento Mori is Latin for "remember that thou art mortal." None of us is leaving this world alive. No matter how much money or power someone possesses, the truth of the matter is, we all meet the same fate. The Stoics believe that we're on loan from nature, and that when we die, we return to it. Keeping this in mind—the undeniable fact that we're all going to die someday, and that today may be our last—evokes our best loving and courageous selves. It makes us more appreciative of the present and all that's contained within it.

If the thought of death brings feelings of fear or sadness, remember that this is just a feeling. It's a value judgment we've placed on the idea of death that we can change. Epictetus said: "It isn't the events itself that disturbs us, but rather our own judgment about them…Death, for example, is not a terrible event…The terror that is evoked within us is evoked from our notion that death is terrible, not from death itself" (*Enchiridion* 5). If we stop seeing death as a looming grim reaper and embrace it as the inevitable destination it is, we take power away from its morbidity. Our impermanence unites us, because inevitable death is something we all have in common.

Memento Mori also helps us prepare for the loss of those we love. This is why it's helpful to appreciate our lives by reflecting not only on our own mortality but also the mortality of those we love. To imagine the death of someone we care about sounds morbid but, again, we're striving to take the "graveness" out of the end of life. There are other schools of philosophy and religions that adopt the practice of this reflection, such as Buddhism. Maranasati is a series of Buddhist meditations on death to cultivate gratitude and take the fear out of dying. Marcus Aurelius also reflected on the mortality of his family and the teachings of Epictetus, writing, "'When you kiss your child,' said Epictetus, whisper to yourself, 'Tomorrow you may die.' One may consider that a bad omen but 'no word is a bad omen,' said Epictetus, 'when it simply conveys something natural. For if that were true, reaping ears of corn would also be a bad omen'" (*Meditations* 11.34.1).

What Epictetus proposes doesn't sound at first like ideal parenting advice. However, he's advising that we acknowledge that we don't know what tomorrow holds. We should love our children each day like it may be the last time we see them. These are the terms in which we live under, for death is simply a consequence of living.

Sometimes the recognition that death will come for us all creates an urgency to pack as much jet-setting and activity into life as possible. The Stoic value of temperance holds that the simple pleasures matter just as much as "bucket list" items. The goal is to be mentally and emotionally present in your life, and to live a life that's guided by purpose and virtue. This way you have no regrets. Death is a natural event and we don't have control over our mortality. This is in agreement with nature. If this feels heavy, heed the perspective of the grim reaper from *Bill and Ted's Bogus Journey*: "You might be a king or a little street sweeper, but sooner or later you dance with the reaper." No one's leaving this bogus journey alive.

The Letting Go Exercise

The Stoics and many other philosophers and spiritual teachers advocated nonattachment, or letting go of the things we can't control or even save from death. This can help us focus on the things we can control and find peace and acceptance when thinking about death. In 12-step recovery groups, the advice often given is to "let go and let god." The Zen proverb is to "let go or be dragged." There's much wisdom in recognizing that whether it's the gods, nature, the universe, or the laws of physics, there is much that's out of our control, and trying to assert control over the forces of the universe is a path to misery. Learning to let go and let natural processes run their course is the way to serenity. Paradoxically, the things we need to let go of the most are often the hardest ones. We're often most bothered by the things we can't control but that directly affect us. For this reason, letting go is an active skill, and for many of us it's something we have to do *over and over*. The mind will naturally move toward trying to solve (and agonize over) unsolvable problems. Over and over we need to learn to turn the mind toward what we *do* have control over.

We can apply this strategy of letting go to the principle of Memento Mori discussed earlier. To do this exercise, start by thinking of a loved one. Then, remind yourself that both they and you will eventually change or pass, as this is nature. Remind yourself that you have no control over this, and that trying to control it will only cause you suffering. Instead, focus on the things you can control. If you practice letting go of people and accept that we're all here for a limited time, it allows you to focus on finding peace in and appreciating the present moment. Yes, it's natural to grieve when the time comes, but having practiced letting go will help you allow in more gratitude than sorrow when you do grieve. This exercise over time will help you remember the impermanence of all things and to let go of the things that cause you suffering. The Buddhist teacher Pema Chödrön is often credited with the quote, "You are the sky. Everything else is just the weather," which elegantly conveys the concept of letting go of the uncontrollable aspects of life that cause us grief.

Chapter 6 Takeaways

- The "view from above" is a Stoic technique for inserting mental space between you and your circumstances, with the goal of obtaining a more effective vantage point from which to approach your problems.

- Being intolerant of distress causes extra distress.

- You can worsen a situation by getting distressed about your distress. For example, you can get depressed about being depressed. This is akin to throwing gasoline on a fire. The way out of this difficulty is to increase your tolerance for discomfort.

- Though counterintuitive, resilience and wisdom are often gained by approaching the things you wish to avoid.

- Premeditatio Malorum is a Stoic practice for coping in advance by mentally rehearsing an upcoming situation and imagining the worst-case outcome. This is different from engaging in unproductive worry, which often focuses on ineffective coping. Instead, this practice involves picturing more effective responses.

- We are all finite. When this notion is salient, your perspective on many things is altered and you often have greater clarity about what really matters and how to live in the present moment.

CHAPTER 7

From Criticism to Compassion: Non-Judgmentalness

Prior to casting judgment upon another person, ask yourself, Which of my own imperfections resembles the one I am about to criticize?

—Marcus Aurelius, *Meditations* 10.30

Chrysippus, the third head of the Stoic school of philosophy, outlines in his book *On Passions* (also translated as *On Emotions* or *On Affections*) how our judgments dictate our emotional reactions. Erroneous judgments can cause emotional reactions that run amok, and one of his strategies was to preemptively deal with these emotions through reason.

It's helpful to understand the Stoic view of emotion. There's the emotion that you feel (happy, sad, angry) and then there's the way you feel about something ("I feel like I can't do anything right" or "I feel like nothing I ever do will be good enough"). When the ancient Stoic philosophers say you can control how you feel, they're speaking about the latter, which is anchored in your interpretation of the situation. The latter (how you feel about a situation, or judgments) also directly affects how a situation makes you feel (emotion), which in turn impacts behavior. Thus, becoming less judgmental is a route to equanimity.

When Epictetus said, "What upsets people is not things themselves, but their judgments about these things," he meant that our judgments can be the source of undue suffering. This can be extended to our interactions with other people and even ourselves. Though Epictetus himself had a rigorous devotion to Stoicism, this didn't mean he had a harsh Stoicism. In fact, he recognized the wisdom of compassion. This is illustrated through his two handles approach (*Enchiridion* 34):

> Each situation offers two handles: one that can uplift and another that can't. When your brother wrongs you, don't clutch the handle of his wrongdoing, as it can't lift. Instead, grasp the handle that reminds you he is your brother, and you share a bond. This is the handle that lifts.

The focus of this chapter is on shifting from using the judgmental handle that will not lift and instead learning to be more compassionate, so we can be more effective. This approach focuses on doing what works. The wise Stoic can apply this two handles approach to themselves as well. Self-criticism and harshness are often the handle that won't carry, but self-compassion is capable of lifting and carrying us as we strive to change our behavior and do better.

What do we learn about the relationship we should have with ourselves from reading the texts of the ancient Stoics? While self-conceit and egomania are incompatible with Stoicism, so too is self-flagellation. Marcus Aurelius's *Meditations* is in some ways his journal, so we can learn more about the relationship he had with himself. While the book is filled with self-critiques, these are all constructive in nature. Aurelius is telling himself that he needs to do better, and he's doing that with temperance and indifference. He's not beating himself down but rather lifting himself up. Ryan Holiday, in *Ego Is the Enemy*, says this too: "Meanwhile, love is right there. Egoless, open, positive, vulnerable, peaceful, and productive" (Holiday 2016, 207).

It's pragmatic to recognize that fallibility is a part of being human. As Epictetus reminds us, "We don't give up on our pursuits because we doubt our ability to perfect and master them" (*Discourses* 1.2.37b). While Stoics strive to emulate the sage, we recognize it's inherently unobtainable. Marcus Aurelius also wrote about trying to improve a situation: "Initiate action, if you have the ability, without concern for whether anyone will take notice. Don't anticipate a grand outcome like Plato's *Republic*; instead, find satisfaction in even the tiniest of successes and recognize their significance" (*Meditations* 9.29).

In developmental psychology, there's a concept of differing parenting styles. People often present a false dichotomy between permissive parenting (warm but lax) and authoritarian parenting (strict but harsh); in reality, there's a third style, authoritative (nurturing yet firm), which tends to be associated with the best outcomes. Stoic wisdom suggests that this supportive yet disciplined approach to a relationship with ourselves is what's needed.

Is Compassion Just?

Toward the end of the twentieth century, the self-esteem movement had become a prominent campaign in the fields of child development and popular psychology. A central idea of these proponents was that you could overcome feelings of inferiority by paying attention to your positive qualities and that increasing your self-worth was associated with a range of positive outcomes. There have been several criticisms of the focus on building self-esteem, which were articulated well by the psychologist Albert Ellis, who wrote, "If you elevate or defame yourself because of your performances, you will tend to be self-centered rather than problem-centered, and these performances will, consequently, tend to suffer" (Ellis 2005, 53). Ellis, known for a direct manner of speaking, continued, "Self-esteem is the greatest sickness known to man or woman because it's conditional." Indeed, scientific investigations have failed to reveal many of the presumed positive outcomes that would result from directly assisting individuals with improving their self-esteem.

Self-compassion has replaced self-esteem as the focus of helping professionals because it produces more favorable results. The main ideas of self-compassion can be viewed through the lens of Stoicism. Modern-day Stoic and cognitive behavioral therapist Donald Robertson (2010) has explained that the virtue of justice can be broken into two components: impartial fairness and benevolent kindness. Therefore, having justice toward ourselves involves being both fair and kind to ourselves. While some might envision Stoics as having a rigid and demanding relationship with themselves, this is a myth and associated with lowercase *s* stoicism. A Stoic life doesn't include being cruel or disrespectful to oneself.

Some people worry that self-compassion breeds complacency, with the idea that we need to kick ourselves in the rear end to get going. While that strategy may work in the short term, it eventually stops working and is a path to being a burnt-out perfectionist. Wisdom calls for us to do what works best in the long run, which is having compassion for ourselves and others. Compassion helps improve performance because it gives us permission to be human. All the energy that would be spent on beating ourselves up can now be spent on doing things we actually care about. Self-compassion helps us take actions that are in line with our values.

Impartial Fairness with Yourself and Others

Social psychologists have identified cognitive fallacies that lead to biased judgments, such as the fundamental attribution error or the actor-observer bias. While there are various iterations, the theme across all of them is that we as humans have a tendency to overgeneralize and label someone based on insufficient data. While a person's behavior is strongly influenced by contextual factors, we create stories about how their behavior is the totality of who that person is. This extreme thinking tends to create extreme emotional responses, which in turn drives extreme behavioral responses. If we're to live a life guided by justice and temperance, then we must learn to have a more nuanced view of ourselves and others.

It can be helpful to think of what's known in psychology as the *state versus trait distinction*. A person can have a depressed mood (state), but that doesn't necessarily mean they're consistently depressed (trait). Person rating is a common cognitive distortion; it involves labeling someone with an overgeneralized description of their personhood. Two main strategies are used to escape this pitfall. The first is judging the person's behavior instead of the person. We might make a mistake, but that doesn't make *us* a mistake. Someone might behave inconsiderately, though this doesn't mean they're on the whole inconsiderate. Judging the behaviors in an interaction helps us focus on improving the situation.

The other main CBT strategy goes a step further. It involves trying to take on an overall attitude of non-judgmentalness. From this perspective, we focus on the facts of the situation instead of our judgments about the person based on our interpretation of an event. A download-able copy of this exercise is available at http://www.newharbinger.com/52663.

Rethinking Judgments

What is a judgment I'm having about myself or someone else?

_____

_____

What experiences are this judgment based on?

_____

_____

_____

Do these experiences and these judgments represent the totality of who the person is in their life?

_____

_____

_____

What pieces of information don't I know about this person?

_____

_____

_____

Are the expectations I have of this person reasonable?

_____

_____

_____

Are there elements from the person's life or history that help explain why they are the way they are?

_____

_____

_____

_____

Is it possible that I'm overgeneralizing from a few instances to create a globalized story about this person?

_____

What are the facts about the situation?

_____

_____

_____

_____

_____

What effect do these judgments have on how I treat this person?

_____

_____

_____

Based on my values, how do I want to treat this person and how would I need to view them to facilitate that behavior?

_____

_____

_____

Is there a more neutral way to restate my judgment?

_____

_____

_____

Questioning our judgments and engaging in compassionate conversations can lead to greater understanding and harmony, both with others and within ourselves. This process holds the potential to yield profound transformations. For instance, two colleagues can have a boisterous argument, clutching on to the same biases they brought into the disagreement, leading nowhere. However, if they engage in a compassionate conversation, intent on understanding each other's perspectives, they can transform their disagreement into a collaborative solution that may actually be of some use.

By questioning our own self-critical judgments, we can cultivate self-compassion and improve our sense of self-worth, leading to a more positive and healthy relationship with ourselves and enabling us to strive for lasting change in both ourselves and society. In other words, we will be motivated, wanting better for ourselves and all of humankind. This turns getting out of bed and facing the day from a dreaded chore to a hopeful and much-anticipated venture.

1. List the label you have for yourself (for example, I'm worthless, stupid, incompetent). You can list more than one, but please only work through the remaining steps one label at a time:

    _____

2. Write out your best argument for why you believe your label is true. Don't hold back. Be as thorough as possible and use additional sheets of paper if necessary.

    _____

    _____

    _____

    _____

    _____

    _____

3. Read through your detailed argument and consider the following:

    •   If you listed specific examples of when you feel you behaved "worthlessly," "stupidly," "incompetently," and so on, is it the case you *always* behave this way? By definition if you characterize yourself as "stupid," for example, then 100 percent of your behavior is stupid.

    •   Is your label true about every facet of your life? Or is it limited to certain areas?

    •   Did you take into account factors outside your control that may have contributed to the circumstances you see as evidence for the label? It might be helpful to review the previous sections on the dichotomy of control in chapter 2.

    •   Is it possible that nuancing your view with phrases such as "I've done some things poorly, but not everything or even most things" or "I have some personal flaws that I'd prefer not to have, but I don't have flaws in every aspect of my life" is more accurate?

- Is it possible you're treating yourself differently than you treat others? For example, do you similarly characterize as "worthless" other people who do some things well and some things not so well?

- Do you tend to notice things that suggest your label is true with relative ease? Do you notice things that suggest it might not be true as easily?

4. Having examined your story about why you believe your label is true, what can you *reasonably* conclude?

_____

_____

_____

_____

Distinguishing Opinions from Facts

It's important to distinguish subjective perceptions from objective facts. It's remarkably easy for humans to understand the difference intellectually but to conflate the two in day-to-day living. We cavalierly say things like "that movie was awful" or "that couch is disgusting." In both cases it can seem we're saying something objective about the movie and the couch. Yet "awful" and "disgusting" aren't actual features of these things, but rather represent our preferences in relation to them. This is easier to see if we apply the "group" test to them. If a group of people viewed the same film, is it a certainty they would all agree that the film was awful? Though it's possible they would share the same opinions of the film, this isn't guaranteed. In contrast, would the same group of people agree that what they're viewing is a movie? There would be consensus because this is an observable fact.

Do you evaluate yourself or others negatively? For example, do you judge yourself to be unattractive, stupid, worthless, or something else? If you do, are those judgments opinions or objective facts? If a group of people looked at you, would they all agree you're unattractive, stupid, or worthless? It may seem like those labels describe your essence, but they're akin to evaluating a movie as awful.

Here's another example: When we purchase a car we have many decisions to make, including the make and model. Working to narrow down our choices, we might next consider things like gas mileage, spaciousness, and how it might fare in an accident. Though ideally we'd prefer it to be strong across all dimensions, more often we must accept trade-offs. For instance, a car that's good in gas mileage might be a smaller, lighter car, making it more likely to be destroyed in an accident. Conversely, a car with a robust exterior might get really poor gas mileage. This is just an example considering only two features. Imagine there were trade-offs on several features, some features are fantastic, some not as great as we'd like but acceptable, and some we might evaluate as awful. Now, how would you characterize the car? Fantastic, neutral, or awful? None of these characterizations would be accurate because your evaluation of the individual dimensions varies. So it is with us and others. Humans have strengths and weaknesses. Thus, it isn't accurate to apply a global label.

The Basis for Compassionate Understanding

Our biology limits our options and shapes our experiences. We will periodically get sick, the frequency of which is in part determined by the body we were born with. Our temperament determines our threshold for experiencing reward and threat, which can be really low or really high, and which directly impacts our emotional life. Paul Gilbert (2009), developer of compassion-focused therapy, emphasizes the poor design of our brains and the mismatch between the environment that selected our brains and our current environment. Evolution has essentially built newer brain structures on top of old ones, a bit like an evolutionary Jenga puzzle, and for an environment containing an abundance of physical threats. It's doubtful scientists would have designed our brains the way they are had they been given the chance. Fortunately, modern life doesn't contain the physical dangers of the past.

Our life is finite and the runway is shorter than we may think. Though none of us can know when we will die, the average human life is 28,835 days. If you're forty years old, you have already spent 14,610 of those days. And there's no guarantee we'll make it to 28,000. Life span is a nonrenewable resource. You didn't have a say in what your biology or life circumstances are, nor how long your life will be. In aggregate, these facts support the conclusion of many philosophers and world religions: Life is difficult. Show yourself and others some compassion for the human predicament.

Cultivating Compassion for Yourself

Now that you have an understanding of compassion for others, extend compassion to yourself with the following visualization. Find a quiet space where you won't be disturbed for at least fifteen minutes. Assume a comfortable position and close your eyes.

Bring to mind a distressing instance in which you've harshly judged yourself. For example, think of a circumstance when you've judged yourself as dumb, inferior, worthless, felt shameful, or something along these lines. Bring forth the entirety of the experience. Observe any physical sensations that are part of this experience. Notice all the feelings that are there. Try to feel them deeply. Take your time. Now, notice the thoughts that participate in this experience. Try to experience your sensations, emotions, and thoughts as if you're in the height of your struggle with them rather than simply recalling them.

Once this experience is fully present for you, work to adopt a compassionate posture with yourself and with the sensations, emotions, and thoughts. Gently remind yourself that you didn't design the brain that's producing these experiences. Recall that you didn't fully orchestrate your life experiences and didn't have a say in the life circumstances you were born into. Use this awareness to respond calmly and fairly to any self-criticism or judgments that are showing up. Watch your judgments and labels come and go as you work to increase your compassionate stance with them.

Next, bring to mind a person you readily have compassion for. See them in your mind's eye as if they were currently in your presence. Allow your compassionate thoughts and emotions toward them to flow into your awareness. Allow yourself to be consumed with compassion.

Now, once again bring to mind the distressing experience, allowing yourself to experience the physical sensations, emotions, and thoughts involved. Once that experience is present for you, expand your awareness to now include the compassionate feelings you brought forth a few moments ago. Expand the reach of this compassion until it captures the person that your mind is judging and criticizing.

Recognizing that our judgments are often subjective assessments rather than objective facts helps us treat others, as well as ourselves, with compassion and empathy. Our ability to cultivate and apply self-compassion redirects our energy toward actions aligned with our values. This is a large building block in the construction of a fulfilling life.

Chapter 7 Takeaways

- Modern science says that the pursuit of self-esteem is ineffective and at times harmful, and that the cultivation of self-compassion is a more effective building block for the life you want.

- Person rating occurs when you overgeneralize, about yourself or others, from small samples of behavior to characterizing someone's overall essence.

- People readily meld their subjective perceptions with objective facts about the world. This tendency pulls you into ineffective person rating and away from compassionate responding.

- Intentionally describing observable events in a matter-of-fact way is a fruitful means of disrupting the human tendency to respond to perceptions as if they were facts.

- The human condition is replete with challenges and argues for a compassionate stance with yourself and others.

CHAPTER 8

Stoic Interpersonal Skills

Always remember that your mission is to be a virtuous human being, staying attuned to nature's expectations. Act without delay, expressing your truth sincerely, but also with kindness, humility, and a commitment to authenticity, devoid of any hypocrisy.

—Marcus Aurelius, *Meditations* 8.5

In their best-selling book *Lives of the Stoics*, Ryan Holiday and Stephen Hanselman (2020) make a fascinating comparison between emperors Marcus Aurelius and Nero. Although both were taught and influenced by Stoic mentors, they became starkly different leaders. Marcus Aurelius was closely mentored by Junius Rusticus, who was heavily influenced by the teachings of Epictetus who came before. When teaching Aurelius, Rusticus found a middle ground between being too passive and too assertive. Aurelius became known as the philosophical emperor, resiliently leading Rome through war and plague.

Nero, on the other hand, was a ruthless and tyrannical emperor. He was advised by Seneca the Younger, one of the most notable Stoic philosophers, having written *Epistulae Morales ad Lucilium* (Moral Letters to Lucilius), which consists of a total of 124 letters. He wrote, "Our suffering is created more in our mind and exists less in reality," an essential idea that helps encapsulate the essence of Stoic philosophy. Unlike Rusticus, Seneca became a paradoxical figure, advocating for the significance of leading a modest Stoic existence while he himself enjoyed a life of opulence and comfort. He was also a more passive counselor, unlike Socrates, who had an overbearing and relentless approach. Socrates would famously accost people and force dialogues, earning him the nickname of "Gadfly," as he seemed to always be buzzing in people's ears. Both Socrates and Seneca the Younger were eventually sentenced to death—Seneca by order of his own pupil, Nero.

What can we draw from the different approaches of Rusticus, Seneca, and Socrates? It is that we must adapt and apply wisdom in a thoughtful and practical manner. If too passive and too aggressive are not effective, Holiday suggests that there's a middle path, and he highlights how Rusticus found a balance of instructing and correcting. Being wise is simply not enough. We must also be tactful in how we impart our wisdom. Modern concepts like assertive communication, healthy boundaries, and interpersonal effectiveness map onto this idea, and this chapter focuses on how to approach these endeavors from a Stoic perspective.

Stoic Interconnectedness

There's a misconception that Stoicism fosters hyper-individualism, regarding oneself as above society and disregarding the notion of acting in accordance with the common good. This isn't the case, however. In fact, the natural tendency of living beings, especially humans, to care for and identify with themselves and then extend this care and identification to other things, including other people, animals, and even aspects of the natural world, is another cornerstone of Stoicism. The ancient Stoics referred to this idea as *oikeiôsis*, "appropriation" or "affinity." The ancient Stoics believed that adopting *oikeiôsis* helps us cultivate empathy and compassion easily. Marcus Aurelius made many references to the importance of working for the common good in *Meditations*. His philosophy recognized the interconnectedness of us all when he said, "What is detrimental to the collective is also detrimental to the individual bee" (*Meditations* 6.54). He believed Stoic virtues working toward the benefit of everyone was the goal of justice: "Life is brief—its fruit consists of a virtuous character and actions that benefit the greater good" (*Mediations* 6.30).

Socrates's form of inquiry, known as the Socratic Method, was born from the lens that we should strive to understand our fellow human beings, as we're all part of the collective. In a society fixated solely on hard work and riches being the ultimate goal—what hyper-individualism promotes—Socrates believed that his divine mission was to observe his fellow citizens and convince them that the utmost good for a person was the well-being of the soul.

Another Stoic philosopher, Hierocles, rendered a series of concentric circles to illustrate *oikeiôsis* and the interconnectedness of humanity (see figure 5). The innermost circle represents the individual; the next circle stands for immediate family and friends. The third circle is extended family and the local community. The fourth circle is the regional and the outermost circle is humanity. Thus, we're all connected to each other. Hierocles's model advocates that we should strive to bolster our interconnectedness by treating each other better. Specifically, he recommended we treat people a little bit better than they deserve.

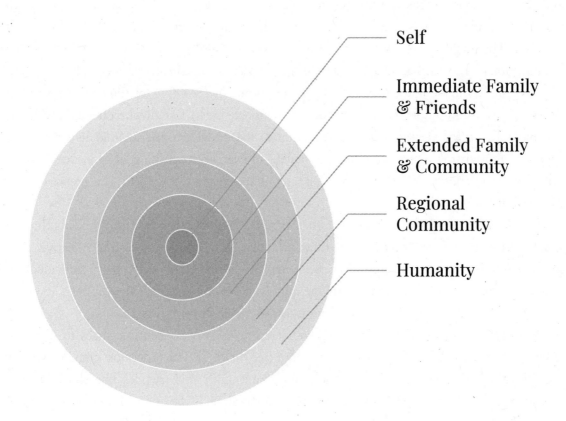

Self

Immediate Family
& Friends

Extended Family
& Community

Regional
Community

Humanity

The Stoic value of justice holds that we should care about the welfare of our fellow humans. This is summarized well with the immortal words from the cult classic *Bill and Ted's Excellent Adventure* where they counsel us to "be excellent to each other." The Golden Rule of treating others how we want to be treated is a universal ideal. Living a Stoic life means treating others according to the virtues of wisdom, justice, courage, and temperance.

Behavior Intolerance: The Frustration That Comes from Acting Outside the Circles of Interconnectedness

Socrates engaged in many famous philosophical debates. Debates with Polus, a young and ambitious student of the Sophist Gorgias, were among these infamous arguments. Gorgias taught rhetoric, the art of persuasive speaking, and so Polus advocated that being a rhetorician is something that everyone should strive for because they're admired and possess much power—that this is a noble goal of life.

Socrates, however, opposed this view and questioned that this was any sort of "power." Polus suggested that power involves persuading individuals to take actions they wouldn't naturally choose. This creates a gap, though, between the rhetorician and the common person, a gap that places the rhetorician in power. But Socrates believed that true power lies in the ability to maintain control and balance over your inner self. This involves practicing self-discipline, living a virtuous life, and achieving a state of contentment where you're not reliant on external factors. This angered and frustrated Polus, who ironically failed to coerce Socrates to adopt his point of view.

In modern cognitive behavior therapy, a common situation is often used to illustrate the connection between how we perceive a situation and how we react. Imagine a scenario where we're driving and someone cuts us off, driving erratically. We must ask ourselves what our response would be. Now, if we imagine that perhaps this individual is rushing to get a family member to the hospital, our response might be compassionate. Reminding ourselves that we don't know the reason the driver cut us off helps us not take it personally and not get angry. The Stoics might say it doesn't matter what the other driver's reason is, because it's out of our control. The other driver may have had rude intentions, and yet we don't want to let that dictate our response in a way where we lose power over ourselves. A key question we must come back to over and over is: "How do we live a just life in a world that's sometimes unjust?" As Socrates told Polus, "It is better to suffer an injustice than to commit one" (Plato's *Gorgias*). Standing in your true power when faced with such situations is to stand inside the circles of interconnectedness and empathy, maintaining self-mastery, virtue, and a sound mind.

In the case of someone not treating you the way you wish to be treated, you must also take inventory of what you can and can't control about the situation. You can put forth your best efforts to rectify the situation by interacting with them (such as having an honest conversation about how you feel and seeking to understand why they're treating you this way). If they don't heed your concern, however, you could remove yourself from the situation. If it's a coworker or family, though, the best option is to continue to act as a wise person—continuing to treat others as you would like to be treated. This isn't to be a doormat. You've expressed your wish to be treated with respect.

A wise person would, again, consider the source. As someone wise, you wouldn't value the actions or opinions of an imprudent person. Though their words may be ignorant, you can decide how you receive them. You can decide whether you believe them or even want to dwell on them. Therefore, you have the choice to decide how (and if) you carry their words with you, which ultimately impacts whether it affects you. This choice is what you have control of in this situation. Marcus Aurelius had this to say about offenses and this choice: "If you decide not to be affected by potential harm, then you won't experience it. If you refuse to acknowledge harm, then you haven't truly been harmed" (*Meditations* 4.7.1).

What about this interaction most upsets me?

_____

_____

_____

What aspects of the situation are under my control?

_____

_____

_____

Does the context and hierarchy of the relationship allow for me to change the interaction? How?

_____

_____

_____

How can I adjust my expectations?

_____

_____

_____

_____

How can I more clearly express what I want and don't want in this situation?

_____

_____

_____

_____

Is the relationship salvageable? _____

What are the pros and cons of tolerating this situation?

_____

_____

_____

What are my options?

_____

_____

_____

Seeing the Relationship from the View from Above

Earlier we discussed the Stoic strategy of gaining perspective by seeing things from a "big picture" perspective. One of the goals of couples therapy is helping people learn to take this view from above together. There's a great deal of emotional intimacy that comes from being able to jointly take this view; accordingly, not every person or relationship will be willing or want to take this vantage with us. From the view from above, we can see that some of the things we squabble about are not actually a huge deal in the big picture.

The concept of the "view from above" or the cosmic perspective is indeed a recurring theme in Stoic philosophy, and it has been attributed to various Stoic philosophers. Taking a view from above helps us see what the real issue is so we can have a constructive dialogue. We can also recognize our preferences and dispreferences and remind ourselves that we can tolerate things not going the way we want. Instead, we can focus our energies on what matters most.

Are You Staying or Going?

From the perspective of a couples therapist, when a couple has reached the point where the relationship is no longer working, there are two possible successful outcomes: the partners improve the relationship to the point where it works for both people or the couple decides to cut their losses and end the relationship. The only bad outcome is things continuing in a state of not working. It takes wisdom and courage to *accept the things we can't change*, which in a relationship could very well be our level of compatibility if we're being our authentic selves.

Many of us run away with the feeling of falling for someone, believing it to be true love. But when this happens, and we expect one thing and the other person does something different, we tend to focus more on the perceived "flaw" than we should; it becomes a bigger deal than it ought to be. Given, not all flaws are created equal and some are definite deal breakers. People often want a list of deal breakers to tell them when to stay or when to go as a way to avoid the emotional labor of making that decision. The truth is, you can leave any relationship for any reason; it's up to you. But it might not be wise to leave any and all relationships that have moments of difficulty.

In weighing this decision, the truism that we typically come back to is that the best predictor of future behavior is past behavior. Comfortable people tend not to change. The timing will never be perfect. Choosing not to decide is still making a decision. Sometimes in life we don't have a good option, so we must choose the least bad option or the option that would be best for us in the long run. Many people stay in relationships that are bad in the long term to avoid the short-term discomfort of leaving their partner. Similarly, many people half commit to a relationship waiting to see if it will improve on its own. We're all on borrowed time, Memento Mori. Nurture healthy relationships and let go of the ones that don't serve you well, so everyone can make the most of their short, precious time.

Epictetus's Two Handles Approach

The two handles approach that we discussed in chapter 7 epitomizes the wise Stoic approach to interpersonal effectiveness, as it focuses on doing what works. To reiterate, in any situation there are multiple ways to approach a problem. Some approaches are more skillful than others. An emotional and vengeful reaction isn't likely to be effective. We must remember that the Stoic value of justice isn't about punishment or vigilantism, it's about impartial fairness and benevolent kindness. We must learn to pause and think before approaching difficult situations and ask ourselves what course of action would be wise. If we can find shared interests and connection, there's an opportunity for collaboration. A downloadable copy of this exercise is available at http://www.newharbinger.com/52663.

Using the Two Handles Approach

Think of an interpersonal situation that is difficult or causing distress and use the two handles approach to resolve it.

What's going on in the situation?

_____

_____

_____

_____

What's my initial emotional reaction?

_____

What can be done to make the situation better?

_____

_____

_____

What could I say or do that would be both fair and kind?

_____

_____

_____

What's the wisest thing I can do in this situation?

_____

_____

_____

_____

How to Apologize

Sometimes apologizing when we make a mistake can be the wisest course of action. It certainly demonstrates temperance and justice, and even requires courage. Of course, we also need to use our wisdom to know whether we actually made a mistake or are falling into a pattern of over-apologizing. A wise Stoic apologies when it's needed. A good apology includes a number of essential components. Consider a time you owed someone an apology and use the framework to consider what you could have said and done.

1. Identify if an apology is warranted.

2. Say sorry genuinely.

3. Own your mistake and take accountability.

4. Recognize their feelings and their suffering.

5. Repair the harm by offering reparations or restitution, if appropriate.

6. Say why it won't happen again.

Developed by Alexis A. Adams-Clark, Xi Yang, Monika N. Lind, Christina Gamache Martin, and Maureen Zalewski. 2022. *DBT Bulletin* 6(1). University of Oregon. Modified and used with permission.

Set Boundaries like a Roman Emperor

Often when we attempt to set boundaries, a sense of guilt initially arises. We lose sight of why we want to set a boundary and put our emotional needs on the back burner; worried the other party may take offense. The guilt can be amplified once the boundary is requested and the other person pushes back. However, it's important to remember what we're essentially saying when we set boundaries. We're telling the other person, "This is what I need to feel safe, valued, and respected." When we read it like that, it becomes an all the more rational request.

The ancient Stoics viewed setting boundaries as part of self-mastery and necessary for the preservation of inner peace. It benefits us to remember this when others push back against our setting limits. When you start setting boundaries, the people who benefited from you not having limits may not like it, and they may push back. They may not respect your boundaries by choosing to believe you won't uphold them. This will make it more difficult to stick to your boundary. Marcus Aurelius felt this pressure too. He often had to remind himself to "emulate the steadfast rocky cape, enduring the ceaseless assault of waves, as it remains unwavering, calming the tumul-tuous waters that surround it" (*Meditations* 4.49).

Externals not within our control, such as how others respond or feel about our request, born of self-preservation and mental well-being, are waves that will always surround us. Being psycho-logically flexible and resilient, we can choose to see that they're still good people, it's just that they simply don't understand. That's okay, and that consideration is granting them the benefit of the doubt. But we still don't have to succumb to being tossed by the waves of their misunder-standing and, perhaps, disagreeable response. The rocky headland doesn't prevent the waves, but it doesn't break for them either. Neither should we. The waters will cease their roar eventually.

Assertive Communication

It's not uncommon for someone to struggle with finding a balance between being too passive and being too aggressive. Assertiveness is a balanced approach. It involves speaking your truth and pursuing what you want, while also maintaining a respectful manner. As psychologist Aaron Beck wrote, "The stronger person is not the one making the most noise but the one who can quietly direct the conversation toward defining and solving problems" (Beck 1989).

Marsha Linehan, the creator of dialectical behavior therapy, developed a framework for assertiveness (Linehan 2014). It involves describing the situation as you see it, expressing how the situation makes you feel, asking for what you want to see happen, and then reinforcing why this will be a good outcome for everyone. Wisdom helps us choose the approach that's most likely to get us what we want while maintaining our self-respect. Consider the example of Miriam and then try this technique for yourself in the following exercise.

Miriam is unhappy with the rut she and her husband have been falling into. She wants to get out more and do fun things together. She finds herself falling into a pattern of complaining about how things are instead of advocating for how she wants them to be. The situation is that the two of them haven't been spending time together in the way they previously did and she misses that. She wants to do more together as a couple because she thinks it'll bring them closer.

Which statement do you think is more likely to get Miriam what she wants?

"You never take me out anymore. Do you even care about me?"

"We haven't been going out as much as we used to and I really miss spending time with you in that way. I want to start doing it again because I think it will be fun and good for us."

What objectively is the situation?

_____

_____

What are my feelings about the situation?

_____

_____

What do I want to see happen?

_____

_____

Why will this be a good thing for everyone?

_____

_____

Saying No

Sometimes the most skillful way to decline an unwanted request is to simply say no without elaboration or excuse. A common interpersonal phenomenon is we want to say no but don't want the other person to be upset, so we come up with a reason to justify saying no. And then the other person will try to problem solve our reasons and an uncomfortable and unpleasant exchange ensues. Consider a salesman who tries to get us to buy something. If we say we can't afford it, they'll likely start talking about financing options. If we say we already have a similar item, they'll likely try to explain why their product is better. But a firm and confident no will be more impactful. For those of us who fall into the pattern of being people pleasers, learning to confidently and calmly say no is a skill we must practice. The more we do it, the easier it gets.

Interpersonal Problem Solving

The Situational Effectiveness Worksheet that follows can be viewed as a culmination of the skills covered in this chapter. The main focus is on what we have within our control to increase our ability to assertively pursue our goals. There are some key questions we can ask ourselves when approaching a situation in which we want to be as skillful as possible:

- How can I approach the situation with wisdom?

- What's the outcome I want from the situation?

- What elements of the situation are within my control?

- What elements of the situation are not within my control?

- How do I want to feel about myself after this interaction?

- Is what I want from the situation possible?

- What do I have to do to get what I want while also maintaining my self-respect and integrity?

You can find a downloadable copy of this exercise at http://www.newharbinger.com/52663.

Situational Effectiveness Worksheet

What was a recent interpersonal interaction that didn't go how I wanted it to?

_____

_____

_____

_____

What was happening in that situation?

_____

_____

_____

_____

What elements of that situation were under my control?

_____

_____

_____

What was the outcome I wanted in that situation?

_____

_____

_____

Is what I wanted realistic?

_____

_____

_____

Within the limits of what was under my control, what would I have had to do to get what I wanted?

_____

_____

_____

What did I learn from this activity that can be applied to future interactions?

_____

_____

_____

_____

_____

Consider the example of Maria, who finds herself in the middle of a family argument.

Maria is in the middle adulthood phase of her life and has been wanting to devote some time during the holidays to her and her children forming new family traditions. This has created conflict with her parents, who want her family to stay involved with the already existing family traditions. As Maria's children get older, she finds herself feeling sadness about this special time in her life slipping away. She feels she can't win: she can either give her parents what they want to keep the peace or defy them and possibly rupture the relationship. As a new Stoic, Maria considers her options because she wants to approach the situation from a place of wisdom. She asks herself:

- How can I approach the situation with wisdom?

  I need to stay calm as I approach this. The anger and passion that come up in me make me want to respond in an emotional way that would be destructive.

- What's the outcome I want from the situation?

  I don't want to lose the special relationships and traditions I have with my larger family, and at the same time I do want to have the ability to set aside time for something special with my own kids.

- What elements of the situation are within my control?

  I'm in control of what I say and how I say it. I can speak with wisdom and I can focus on the common good.

- What elements of the situation are not within my control?

  I'm not in control of how my parents respond or what their expectations are of me.

- How do I want to feel about myself after this interaction?

  I want to be able to feel like I'm still a loving daughter and a loving mother.

- Is what I want from the situation possible?

  I'm not sure. I know that it's possible for me to speak with my parents in a loving and respectful way about the situation. I don't know if I can control their reaction. But I'm sure there's some room for compromise. I want them to be happy and they want me to be happy.

- What do I have to do to get what I want while also maintaining my self-respect and integrity?

  I need to approach this in a nuanced way. I can't approach this from a place of antagonism where I see it as either them getting what they want or me getting what I want. I need to speak with love and appreciation for the larger family culture and tradition. And I need to make space for me to step into the role of the future matriarch of my own family. Perhaps I can ask them how they navigated this earlier in their lives. Previously, everything they did was with my mother's parents, and at some point it shifted for them. If I can talk with them about how they navigated that, perhaps I can increase their empathy for my situation and learn from their experiences in a way that's collaborative.

By evaluating what we can and can't control in a situation we can focus our efforts on being skillful as we attempt to overcome the interpersonal challenges in our life. This can help us act in a manner that's wise and in keeping with our personal values.

Chapter 8 Takeaways

- Stoicism is a philosophy that involves caring about other people and participating in society.

- Relationships are complex and you can benefit from a range of skills that help you manage them effectively. These include being able to effectively ask for what you want and to say no when needed.

- Relationships are another context in which being mindful of the Stoic concept of dichotomy of control enhances your effectiveness.

- We're all interconnected. The Stoic strives to behave in ways that are best for the "beehive."

CHAPTER 9

Learning to Think like Socrates: Overcoming Double Ignorance

*While you may not be a Socrates yet, strive to live as someone
who aspires to be a Socrates.*

—Epictetus, *Enchiridion* 51

Socrates's teaching method of asking questions, instead of simply lecturing, was a paradigm shift that has stood the test of time. His journey that would lead him to become one of the most revered philosophers of all time began when Chaerephon (a philosopher and loyal friend) asked the all-knowing Oracle at Delphi who was the wisest of men. The Oracle replied, "There is none wiser than Socrates." In acknowledgment of his own ignorance, Socrates didn't believe it. He set out to prove the Oracle wrong by finding someone wiser than himself, and instead he found that the people who professed to know things were actually ignorant. Worse yet, they were unaware of their own ignorance. He said, "There exists only one virtue, wisdom, and one vice, ignorance" (Diogenes Laertius, *Lives of Eminent Philosophers*).

Although Socrates himself left behind no written works, his legacy is carried on in the works of his students, such as Plato and Xenophon. Plato would write the account of the most recalled legal defense in world history, *The Apology of Socrates*. Stoics such as Epictetus and Marcus Aurelius also wrote about him. Though Socrates predated the Stoics, he's considered to be the grandfather of Stoicism, and his commitment to living a life of virtue makes his teachings highly compatible with Stoicism. After all, the essence of the Stoic virtues are wisdom and wisdom in action.

The focus of this chapter is the core of the teachings of Socrates, seeking wisdom and striving to overcome our own ignorance. The line "The more I learn, the more I realize how much I don't know" is often attributed to the great mind of Albert Einstein. Alternatively, we might say that "people don't know what they don't know." Socrates would call this "not knowing what we don't know" *double ignorance*, and much of his work was dedicated to overcoming this within himself and those around him.

There are stories we tell ourselves out of habit that don't always reflect reality. Learning to think like Socrates involves mentally taking a step back and taking a good hard look at our thought processes, assumptions, and behavior patterns.

What Are Underlying Assumptions?

A basic concept of philosophy and psychology is that while objective reality exists, we tend to experience our own interpretation of that reality based on our history, assumptions, mood, culture, and a variety of other factors. Social psychology teaches us that people tend to see what they expect to see, and tend to interpret their perceptions in a manner that's consistent with their expectations as well. Also, mood-dependent memory is a real thing, making it hard for us to remember the full story. Because of this, our skewed narratives can be self-sustaining if left to their own devices.

Socrates attributed his wisdom to the awareness of his own ignorance. Even at the end of his life, he was still seeking to overcome this. Seeking to recognize and overcome our own blind spots is an important and ongoing process. To follow in his footsteps, it's imperative that we observe and study our own minds. There's consensus that there are thought processes that occur within our awareness and thought processes that happen just outside of our awareness but that are accessible. A key early step in cognitive behavioral therapy is learning to mentally decelerate and identify the cognitions that occur just outside of our awareness and impact what we feel and what we do.

Here's a thought experiment. For this exercise, hold off on looking up the answer on the internet and instead use this as an opportunity to practice identifying underlying assumptions. Imagine a child asking their parent, "Is a fox a cat or a dog?" To answer this the parent might consider a few questions, such as:

- What are some of the differences between dogs and cats?

- Is a fox big like a dog or small like a housecat?

- Can both foxes and wolves be dogs?

- If a puma is a cat and a wolf is a dog, which is a fox more like?

- If cats purr and dogs bark, what sound does the fox make?

- Why does a fox have both cat eyes and canine teeth?

- How come some foxes can climb trees?

When faced with a question we don't know the answer to, paying attention to our reasoning patterns and how we try to go about solving the problem can teach us about our underlying assumptions. Now, if you're a biologist or zoologist, you will most likely know that foxes are part of the Canidae family of animals, which makes them canines (dog family).

The point is, we all have hidden assumptions and learning to identify them takes practice. Let's start with an example that isn't emotionally laden. There's a minor controversy in the food world related to the question of whether pineapple belongs on a pizza. You might not have a strong opinion on this, but for the exercise, pick "yes" or "no."

1. Does pineapple belong on pizza? (yes/no)

2. Take it a step further and explore the reasons for your opinion.

3. What are the reasons why pineapple does or doesn't belong on a pizza?

If we were to ask this question of Socrates, his first response might be to ask what pizza is. The idea of it might not be so foreign to him. It's rumored that the ancient Greeks did make a flatbread called *plakous* that was flavored with toppings like herbs, onion, cheese, and garlic. However, the philosopher's question can also illustrate wisdom. The answer to "Does pineapple belong on pizza?" is informed by first exploring how we define the concept of pizza.

Similar dialogues could be had for questions like "Can a country music song feature an electric guitar?" or "Is a hot dog a sandwich?" An interesting example is that of when the American fast food giant Taco Bell tried opening up their restaurants in Mexico. They were met with confusion because the menu was so different from that of the local authentic taquerias. A Socratic line of questioning might have asked, "What does it mean to be a taco?" or better yet, "What does it mean to be a Crunchwrap Supreme?"

Socratic Approaches to Group Discussions

Another place to practice your Socratic skills are group settings. If you find yourself teaching a class or leading a group, you might use it as an opportunity to explore the content instead of lecturing. You might imagine a group dialogue on the merits of pineapple on pizza using the format below. The use of Socratic strategies can be different in group settings, but the overall goal of trying to seek wisdom and overcome ignorance remains while also trying to foster group curiosity and collaboration. You can find a downloadable copy of the following guide at http://www.newharbinger.com/52663.

Quick Guide: Socratic Questioning for Group Discussions

The Socratic Method is a process of breaking things down and putting them together in a new way. It's a process of thinking *with* people instead of thinking *for* them. In a group format, this means 1) breaking it down (discussing what the material is saying), 2) evaluating what's being said, 3) expanding on that by folding in other perspectives, 4) putting it all together for a more robust perspective, and 5) creating actionable strategies to apply in reality.

1. Breaking It Down

"What do we think they're saying here?"

"What's the main point they're making?"

"Are there any real-world examples of what they're talking about?"

2. Evaluating What's Being Said

"Why is this important?"

"What does this look like in real life?"

"In your experience, is what they're saying true?"

"How can this help us as we work toward our goals?"

3. Expanding with Other Perspectives

"Is there anything they're missing?"

"Are there other ways to look at this?"

"Are there cultural perspectives that can add to the conversation?"

"Can we add more nuance to make this more accurate?"

4. Putting It All Together

"How can we restate the idea in a way that captures everything we've discussed?"

5. Creating Actionable Strategies

"How can we try this out this week?"

Socrates and Pseudo-Socrates

There are some contemporary figures who might identify with Socrates, though he would likely not identify with them. In his time, there were Sophists, who would lecture or teach for money. They would often teach others how to use logic or reason to win arguments, even unjust ones. Socrates was highly critical of this group, as he noted that they were more interested in money than virtue and they tended to use reason to tell people what they wanted to hear instead of what was true. This is readily apparent in modern law and politics, where people try to use reason to justify their assertions, instead of using reason to question their beliefs and possibly arrive at a better understanding of the truth. In this way, reason can be used to fortify ignorance.

In Plato's *Gorgias*, a dialogue between Socrates and Polus, they discuss the value of rhetoric (persuasion). Socrates makes his views plainly known, saying that this manner of using reason as a means of persuasion was often "guesses at what's pleasant with no consideration for what's best." In other words, simply because it sounds convincing doesn't mean it's true or just. Learning to think like Socrates is less about how to win arguments and more about how to overcome ignorance and seek wisdom.

The Socratic Method

The *elenchus* (or *elenctic*) method is a Socratic manner of dialogue where both parties ask and answer questions to uncover each other's underlying assumptions. In looking at the original Socratic dialogues, a pattern is readily observed. Socrates typically asks the other party to define the construct they're discussing. He'll espouse some ignorance on the subject and ask questions to first test the limits of this definition. After the construct has been explored, he then tests the consistency of the argument with the construct they have defined. The dialogues often end in a state of *aporia* (puzzlement or uncertainty), as the initial assumption being tested proves to have some ignorance or conceit of knowledge. Today, therapists carry the process a few steps further, and the next chapter will focus on a framework that integrates ancient Socratic wisdom and modern cognitive behavioral practice. For now, let's focus on understanding the fundamentals of Socrates's methodology.

An amusing example of the Socratic Method can be found in Xenophon's *Symposium*, where Socrates is having a beauty contest with another man, Critobulus. Now, Socrates was famously not a prototypical example of the ancient Greek ideal of male beauty. He was balding, with bulging eyes and an upturned nose. Socrates began the beauty contest by asking his competitor to define the term "beauty." He then worked to expand that definition by asking questions such as whether only humans could be beautiful. The answer was that animals and even objects such as a spear or shield could be beautiful. When Socrates probed this answer it was stated that if something was well made for its function, it could be beautiful as well. Socrates seized on this. He asked about the purpose of eyes and the answer was to see; he then said that his bulging crablike eyes were better able to see than his competitor's. He also noted that his upturned nose didn't obstruct his vision and his open nostrils easily could catch scents and that these further must be a sign of beauty.

Although this dialogue has the flavor of two guys jesting out of boredom, it does illustrate the Socratic Method in a very accessible way. To answer a question, we must first understand what exactly we're asking. In our therapist manual, *Socratic Questioning for Therapists and Counselors*, we note that distorted thoughts are often based on distorted definitions. Socrates would always focus on deconstructing and delving into the definition before trying to answer the question. He never wrote a manual for his method, so we have to try to recreate it by studying the ancient dialogues. Here is a rough outline of his typical approach:

1. *Identify the Proposition:* What's the question being asked?

2. *Identify the Key Concept:* What's the key concept for that question?

3. *Define the Construct:* What's the operationalization of this concept?

4. *Test the Construct:* What are the limits of this definition?

5. *Test for Consistency:* How does the refined definition compare to the original proposition?

The beauty contest dialogue can be used to illustrate this methodology.

1. Identify the Proposition: What's the question being asked?
   Who is more beautiful, Socrates or Critobulus?

2. Identify the Key Concept: What's the key concept for that question?
   Beauty

3. Define the Construct: What's the operationalization of this concept?

    The initial definition is about being aesthetically pleasing.

4. Test the Construct: What are the limits of this definition?

    Beauty can be observed in animals and even man-made objects. It must also mean being well made for the function of the item.

5. Test for Consistency: How does the refined definition compare to the original proposition?

    Beauty might not be as narrow as initially defined, and functionality might be as important as aesthetics.

Admittedly, the beauty contest is a silly example. How might this Socratic Method apply to more important matters? Consider the following examples.

Example A

1. Identify the Proposition: What's the question being asked?

    My business idea failed. Am I a failure?

2. Identify the Key Concept: What's the key concept for that question?

    Being a failure

3. Define the Construct: What's the operationalization of this concept?

    The initial focus might be on the fact that a failure was experienced with overgeneralization. This leads to the false impression that the failure makes up the totality of who the person is.

4. Test the Construct: What are the limits of this definition?

    Does failing once make someone a failure for the rest of their life? For everyone who is successful, have they always been successful, with no history of failing? If someone fails once and then goes on to succeed later on, are they a failure or a success?

5. Test for Consistency: How does the refined definition compare to the original proposition?

    Failure is an experience, not an identity. We can fail and go on to succeed later. Our setbacks don't have to define us.

Example B

1. Identify the Proposition: What's the question being asked?

   Why is it that no matter how much I achieve, it never feels like I'll be good enough?

2. Identify the Key Concept: What's the key concept for that question?

   Being good enough

3. Define the Construct: What's the operationalization of this concept?

   Being good enough is a "moving target." I don't really know what it means or what it would look like. I suppose it means I'd finally feel satisfied and proud of myself.

4. Test the Construct: What are the limits of this definition?

   In your mind is there an achievement that you think would make you feel good enough? Have you ever thought about prior achievements? If those didn't leave you feeling fulfilled, why do you think this next hurdle will fill the void? Could you find satisfaction if you never reached perfection? Is it possible that you're trying to find self-acceptance through achievement? Is being good enough something that has to be earned? If we were to go to a maternity ward and see all the babies there, could you tell them that they weren't good enough because they have yet to achieve anything with their lives?

5. Test for Consistency: How does the refined definition compare to the original proposition?

   Maybe being good enough isn't something you have to wait to achieve. Perhaps if you keep doing your best, your best will get better and that's okay.

Try the Socratic Method on Yourself

The next step in learning to think like Socrates is practicing this method on yourself using the following exercise. It's best to start with things that you don't have an overly strong opinion about. Start with less emotional topics before moving on to your more central assumptions. Another lesson to be learned from the life of Socrates is that generally people won't like it if you accost them with these questions. Focus on applying them to yourself and practicing the skills. You can find a downloadable copy of this exercise at http://www.newharbinger.com/52663.

Learning the Socratic Method

1. Identify the Proposition: What's the question being asked?

   _____

   _____

2. Identify the Key Concept: What's the key concept for that question?

   _____

3. Define the Construct: What's the operationalization of this concept?

   _____

   _____

4. Test the Construct: What are the limits of this definition?

   _____

   _____

   _____

5. Test for Consistency: How does the refined definition compare to the original proposition?

   _____

   _____

   _____

   _____

The next chapter will focus on building on these core skills to apply the Socratic Method to our self-limiting beliefs. Practice the skills in this chapter until you find yourself having some confidence in your ability to identify thoughts and question the assumptions that underlie those thoughts. If you are working with a coach or therapist, you might spend a few weeks on the skills contained in this chapter; you can't skip the fundamentals.

Chapter 9 Takeaways

- Being ignorant of your own ignorance is the first hurdle to overcome.

- In overcoming your own ignorance, you learn to identify and question your assumptions.

- Ancient Socratic wisdom is compatible with modern cognitive behavioral therapy.

- It's not only what happens but also your interpretation of what happens that guides how you feel and what you do.

- You can learn to examine your own thoughts and perceptions by using the Socratic Method.

- It's advisable to begin using this practice first on things you don't feel too strongly about, before moving on to your more central assumptions.

CHAPTER 10

A Self-Socratic Method: Using Socratic Thinking to Get Unstuck

Wonder is the sentiment of a philosopher, and the journey of philosophy commences with wonder.

—Socrates, Plato's *Theaetetus*

Wisdom is born of admitting there are things you may not know, awareness of your own inexperience, and gaps in knowledge. The previous chapter focused on meta-cognitive skills applied to thoughts and assumptions that are not emotionally laden. Typically, the painful self-limiting beliefs we have are more of a process to shift, and so having a good grasp on the foundational skills, the basics, is recommended. Often, people need to practice the skills from the previous chapter over a period of time before advancing to this final chapter.

A lawyer might focus on using Socratic questioning to assess for consistency in an argument or a testimony. Typically, there's a process of open- and close-ended questions to establish what's being evaluated and then close-ended questions to test the consistency of the argument or perspective. This would be referred to as an *elenctic* method (or *elenchus*). Alternatively, a therapist may use a different type of Socratic questioning to help with evaluating the self-narrative and discovering unknown or hidden truths. Socrates's mother (named Phaenarete) was a midwife, and Socrates viewed his work and methods as being a midwife for thought. This philosophical midwifery method of helping someone "give birth" to a new thought of their own (as opposed to telling them what to think) is called the *maieutic* method. This chapter will cover strategies from both methods.

Psychotherapeutically, the goal of Socratic questioning is to think *with* the client as opposed to thinking *for* them. This joint process begins with decelerating thought, pausing, and being in the present moment. Then we take a step back from these current thoughts. Here, having achieved some distance from being consumed by thought, we can effectively seek to understand things as they are, expanding our awareness with curiosity. Then we can begin to synthesize the information into a more balanced perspective. These are also the steps an individual can use to apply a *Self-Socratic Method* of inquiry to get unstuck in their lives. If you can get enough cognitive distance to see your own thought processes, and then take another step farther from these processes to observe that you're in fact noticing them, this is what we call the *observing mind* or *observing self*.

This observing self can be a key collaborator in the application of Socratic inquiry to your own mental processes and belief structures, so you can serve as your own philosophical midwife as you seek to evaluate your assumptions. In instances where it's hard to get unstuck on your own, working with a professional might be helpful. You can find a downloadable copy of the following summary of the Self-Socratic Method at http://www.newharbinger.com/52663.

Self-Socratic Method

The Self-Socratic Method encompasses the following steps:

1. **Focusing:** First, identify what to focus on. What are the fears that keep you stuck? What are your self-limiting beliefs and assumptions?

2. **Understanding:** Next, explore the context and origin of those assumptions. What's the origin of these beliefs? What context did they develop in? What behavior patterns accompany these beliefs? Are there any vicious cycles?

3. **Curiosity:** Expand your awareness with curiosity and exploration. If you mentally take a step back, what perspectives are you missing? Is there missing context? What are the gaps in knowledge? Are there things you know that you're forgetting? Are there important experiences you've yet to have because of your avoidance or control strategies?

4. **Summary and Synthesis:** Finally, summarize and synthesize the inquiry to develop a new perspective. How can you pull it all together to create a balanced point of view? How can you put your new perspective into practice? What do you still need to learn or test out?

Step 1: Focusing

The first step in this process is choosing what to evaluate. An effective Socratic dialogue will be focused on evaluating one premise at a time. When people think about their problems and their self-narrative, they often do it in a nonlinear manner. This nonlinear approach leads us to engaging in *rumination*.

Rumination can be understood by thinking about how a ruminative digestive system works (such as in a cow). A cow partially digests something, vomits it up, chews on it again, swallows it down, partially digests it again, and cycles through this to digest things that typically would be difficult for you or I to digest. Humans mentally do this with painful or self-limiting beliefs. When a situation doesn't seem to make sense, it's of course very unpleasant. People tend to think about the situation over and over again, believing that this approach will surely bring some clarity.

However, research shows that when people do this, they tend to focus on the story in an uneven manner. This is where different ideas and different experiences get jumbled together. In fact, this jumbling often leads to a reconsolidation of the memory, where the memories and beliefs tend to become more extreme. That is to say, rumination tends to lead to a more extreme self-narrative. To avoid this pattern of rumination, it's helpful to pick one thing at a time.

Know Thyself

Although you will likely have done some introspection prior to this, take a moment to inventory some assumptions you might not be aware of.

What are some of the major relationships I have in my life?

_____

_____

_____

From those relationships, what have I learned about myself, others, and the world in general?

_____

_____

_____

What are some of the major experiences in my life that have shaped who I am and my assumptions?

_____

_____

_____

From those experiences, what assumptions did I learn about myself, others, and the world in general?

_____

_____

_____

Are there other major factors that have shaped who I am (including cultural and intercultural messaging)?

_____

_____

_____

From those factors, what messages did I learn about myself, others, and the world in general?

_____

_____

_____

Do any of these assumptions seem to keep you stuck or from engaging in the type of life you want to be living? You may already know what you want to evaluate. If you do, write it down to help you stay focused. If you're not sure what you want to evaluate yet, that's completely fine, and the next section will help you identify which of your assumptions to explore. Even if you know what you want to explore, the next section will help you develop a better understanding of the underlying assumptions to give you a more productive line of Socratic inquiry.

Gathering Data

This stage often involves an empowering tool known as *self-monitoring*. This puts you in the captain's chair, with the ability to properly examine why your beliefs exist and how they affect your present struggles. Human memory isn't entirely reliable, and can also be distorted by stress, insomnia, anxiety, mood, chronic pain, burnout, relationship difficulties, and more. As the saying goes, "A dull pencil is better than a sharp mind." So, it's important to do some data tracking (and recording) to learn more about the assumptions that underlie your distress.

To do this, you first must track when that specific distress occurs, when it's the strongest, and which situations tend to evoke it. This can include internal and external stimuli. Typically, it's helpful to describe which specific emotion is tied to that distress, and to rate the intensity of the emotion to see which situations may be the best clues to investigate. To help learn this process, we'll follow the story of Dan as he explores his feelings of being a failure. Subsequently, space will be provided for you to explore your own self-narrative.

Situation Who, what, when, and where?	External Context What's happening around me in this situation?	Internal Context What's happening internally in this situation? Where is my attention? What thoughts are going through my head?	Emotion and Intensity What am I feeling? On a scale of 1 to 100, how intensely am I feeling it?
By myself, preparing a presentation, Monday morning, at work	Everyone else seems really productive and confident.	I'm panicking. I'm sure I'm going to blow this presentation. I don't think I can do this. I'm worried about losing my job. I can't focus. I just keep thinking about what a failure I am.	Fear 85

With my partner, making dinner, at night, at home	They're asking me how my day was, and I don't want to talk about it. They're trying to make small talk and I'm being kind of rude to them for no good reason.	I don't want to talk about work. I don't want to think about work. Thinking about work reminds me how much of a failure I feel like I am. I feel anxious but I have a hard time bringing it up with my partner. I don't want to be rude to them, but I also don't want to break down and show them how scared I feel. I just want it all to go away.	Fear 50 Irritability 90
By myself, doom-scrolling on my phone, later that night, on the couch	My partner said I was being rude and they left me home alone.	I'm relieved to not talk about work but worried about my relationship. I'm mad at myself for creating problems at home. Now I'm stressed and worried about home and work.	Fear 70 Irritability 70

What themes do I notice?

I tend to panic, but I don't talk to anyone about it. In trying to avoid thinking about what's bothering me I make a new problem (that's probably a bigger problem).

In what external situations are these sensations most intense?

Situations where I might screw up or look like an idiot.

What internal circumstances tend to make it worse?

Avoidance. I avoid dealing with the problem and it only gets worse.

Now try filling one out on your own. Keep in mind that the worksheet isn't magic, and there's no need for perfectionism. If something useful gets written down and placed in the wrong column or row, that's still helpful. What's most important is capturing the data. Later we will analyze it.

Situation Who, what, when, and where?	External Context What's happening around me in this situation?	Internal Context What's happening internally in this situation? Where is my attention? What thoughts are going through my head?	Emotion and Intensity What am I feeling? On a scale of 1 to 100, how intensely am I feeling it?

What themes do I notice?

In what external situations are these sensations most intense?

What internal circumstances tend to make it worse?

Track this over time because some weeks may be atypical in the challenges you face. As you gather data across a week or several weeks, you'll also accumulate themes. You can use these themes to get a better idea of what to explore. While some of the thoughts that go through our minds are just noise or nonsense, if we track the themes of our thoughts, we can get a better idea of the underlying stories we have developed about ourselves and the world around us (see figure 6). Our underlying self-limiting beliefs and assumptions influence the rules we create for ourselves, the predictions we make, and how we interpret what happens. Learning to identify our underlying beliefs is a process.

Surface-Level Thoughts

Assumptions and Rules

Underlying Beliefs and Assumptions

Someone has an ongoing thought process that their family doesn't like them, and this often causes incredible sadness. What are the assumptions that underlie the interpretation that could be driving that sadness? For example, maybe the person extrapolates from this interpretation that they're unlikable as a person or that no one will ever love them. This self-narrative of unlikability might speak to why the person arrives at such great distress from that situational interpretation.

In another example, someone who is considering leaving a codependent relationship might have distressing thoughts that the other person won't be able to cope without them. Underlying this distressing thought might be the assumptions that it's their job in life to take care of other people, and that it would be selfish of them to leave.

What are the common themes of my assumptions?

_____

_____

_____

_____

_____

What situations tend to be difficult for me?

_____

_____

_____

_____

_____

In those situations, what do I typically think, feel, and do?

_____

_____

_____

_____

_____

What's my typical interpretation of those situations?

_____

_____

_____

What are possible reasons these situations might bring up these thoughts and emotions for me?

_____

_____

_____

_____

What assumptions might underlie those situations?

_____

_____

_____

_____

_____

Do those assumptions hold constant across situations?

_____

_____

_____

If you have a hard time articulating or identifying the underlying assumptions, one philosophical midwife strategy is something called the *downward arrow technique*. This is a delving strategy that asks: If the surface-level thought were true (hypothetically), why does your interpretation result in the emotion you're experiencing? Where the interpretation and the emotion overlap is your underlying beliefs.

Why does my interpretation of the situation cause me to have this specific emotional reaction?

_____

_____

_____

_____

What possible assumptions might explain my reaction?

_____

_____

_____

Do these assumptions appear to be central to my challenges?

_____

_____

_____

It's worth noting that this process can take a good deal of time. Don't be discouraged if you're not able to instantly identify what your underlying assumptions are. This is often something people need to track over time and meditate upon. While you're working to identify what your underlying assumptions are, it's a good time to practice the Stoic skills and strategies introduced in the earlier chapters.

Believability of the Assumption

After you identify the assumption that underlies your distress, take a moment to ask yourself how much you believe this assumption. If you find that the assumption is something that's distressing but also nonsensical (meaning you don't intellectually or emotionally believe it), then the best strategy might be to reorient your attention to living a life guided by your values and the Stoic virtues.

Demandingness and Assumptions

One of the first applications of Stoic philosophy into cognitive therapy was done by the famous psychologist Albert Ellis. He focused on the underlying irrationality of our assumptions, such as hidden demandingness or frustration intolerance. Ellis once summarized some of his observations with the following guidance for evaluating our assumptions: "There are three musts that hold us back: I must do well. You must treat me well. And the world must be easy" (Ellis 2005).

A good Stoic life isn't one that's free from challenges or obstacles. People develop unnecessary suffering when they have rigid demands for life that are not in keeping with the principles of reality. If your assumption is something that you deem a *should* or a *must*, it's likely that it will cause you great distress. Rigidity is the core problem. Assumptions regarding the way things should be done or how other people should behave often drive misery. You will be trying to control things you're unable to control. It may be important to review the early chapters on Stoic philosophy to help defuse demandingness.

A common observation is that many people have good reasons for these "should" statements. For example, in many places it's a law that the inside lane on a freeway is for passing, and that therefore you should move out of the way if someone wants to pass you. This is an example of a situation where you might have a good reason for your assumption, and rigidly holding on to this will likely increase misery because the world doesn't run on reason. Fighting against reality from a place of nonacceptance often creates a disproportionate response that makes it hard to be effective. The Stoic perspective is to focus on what you have control over. If an assumption that people should drive courteously is associated with a strong emotional response (such as anger), then you might assess whether there's more to the assumption, such as "Other people should drive courteously and if they don't I'll punish them" or "Other people should drive courteously and if they don't I can't stand it." Assumptions that focus on elements out of your control can distract you from the elements of the situation that are within your control.

Examining Your Definition

Socrates often used his methods to evaluate virtues and ethics. Prior to this he would work to define the term being evaluated. If we're to evaluate whether something is virtuous first, we must define virtuous. If we're to evaluate whether something is ethical, we must define ethics. Similarly, if we're to apply this Socratic manner of thinking to our self-limiting beliefs and narratives, then we must define what it is we're evaluating.

For example, consider a person with a belief that they're a bad mother. Before we can get into evaluating that, we would need to look at their understanding of what it means to be a good mother. In this instance, there's good data that it's impossible to be a perfect mother, and that often a healthier and more realistic goal is to be a "good enough" mother. This mother evaluating the expectations they place on themself (and that others have placed on them) can allow for an initial inquiry of "What's the goal?" Often our distress doesn't just come from our assumptions but is driven by the assumptions (or definitions) within our assumptions. The question (or a variant of the question) "How good is good enough?" is often a key component of this process.

Another example is if someone has a belief that they're a failure or has a fear of failing. First it would be important to evaluate how they define failure. If that individual defines failure as any instance of failing, then it will be impossible for them to not be a failure, as it's impossible in life to only have successes. Many people instead define perseverance and grit as being the key attributes in regard to success and not failing.

A third example is if someone has a belief that they're unlovable. There are a number of assumptions that need to be examined. First, is it possible for a human being to be unlovable? At what age does this begin? Is it possible for an infant to be born unlovable? Is the love you receive an accurate measure of the love you deserve? Often there's a false equivalency of the value that others place on you and your intrinsic value as a human being.

Our definitions tend to lean in the direction of our emotions. Therefore, it's important to set a universal definition that applies to everyone to help balance out cognitive filtering. Take a moment to consider the assumption you're evaluating and consider how you're defining the term. It might be helpful to look it up in a dictionary. If the term is an absolute, break it down into a continuum and establish a cutoff point that's "good enough."

What am I evaluating and how am I defining it?		
My fear that I'm a failure. If I make a mistake, it's a failure and that makes me a failure.		
Is my definition realistic?	Yes	(No)
Is my definition universal (same standards for myself as other people)?	Yes	(No)
Is my definition setting me up for disappointment?	(Yes)	No
Is there a more balanced or reasonable alternative definition I could consider?	(Yes)	No
Working definition for the inquiry:		
Failure means quitting because I'm afraid instead of making a mistake. I can't be successful if I'm afraid of making mistakes.		

What am I evaluating and how am I defining it?		
Is my definition realistic?	Yes	No
Is my definition universal (same standards for myself as other people)?	Yes	No
Is my definition setting me up for disappointment?	Yes	No
Is there a more balanced or reasonable alternative definition I could consider?	Yes	No
Working definition for the inquiry:		

Step 2: Understanding

The next step in our Self-Socratic Method of inquiry is to develop an understanding of how the assumption formed and is currently reinforced in your life.

Is this something someone has specifically said to me in the past? If so, who?

_____

Is this something I inferred? If so, how?

_____

_____

Can I trace the origin of this assumption?

_____

_____

_____

_____

_____

_____

Experiences

If this assumption is something you have carried with you in your life, as if your mind is a backpack, can you remember where you picked it up? Did you find it on your own? Was it given to you? Is this something you acquired in a single experience or that developed over time? In the next exercise, write down what you remember about the origin of this assumption. This can be an emotionally difficult process, and you might need to pace yourself. The goal of this isn't to write out a trauma narrative but rather to speak generally about how this assumption may have developed.

The origin of my assumption:

The first memory I have related to my fear of failure is the feeling growing up that nothing was ever good enough for my dad. I remember working hard at school and showing him my grades, and he was never impressed. I remember trying hard at sports and he never came to watch me. It just felt like nothing I did was good enough.

The origin of my assumption:

_____

_____

_____

_____

_____

Evidence

It's important to consider whether there are other pieces of evidence to support the assumption. Be careful here to not try to use one thought or assumption as evidence of another thought or assumption. This is a place to consider facts. Other important assumptions might come up, and if that's the case, you can write them down and evaluate them next. They likely deserve their own evaluation.

Are there facts or pieces of evidence to support the assumption being evaluated?

The main evidence to support my fear of being a failure is my lack of achievement. I've had some setbacks in my life. My avoidance and procrastination have led to me getting in trouble at work before. I was fired once for it. One time I was going to be fired but I quit before they could fire me. So there are instances where I do feel like I've actually failed in a way that resulted in my being terminated.

Are there other facts or pieces of evidence to support the assumption being evaluated?

_____

_____

_____

_____

_____

_____

Summarize the Case for the Assumption

Finally, you'll want to summarize the case to support the assumption you're evaluating.

What's a summary of the case to support the assumption being evaluated?

The assumption that I'm a failure is based on early interactions I had with my father. In these interactions I always had the impression that nothing I ever did was good enough for him. The current support for my being a failure is my lack of successes or major achievements. Also, my procrastination and avoidance have resulted in job loss and job problems before.

What's a summary of the case to support the assumption being evaluated?

_____

_____

_____

_____

_____

_____

Step 3: Curiosity

After you develop a working understanding of the assumption you're evaluating, and the case to support that assumption, it's time to expand your awareness with curiosity. It's important to know what you're missing.

Is There Missing Context?

Often, we develop situation-specific interpretations that we then generalize beyond the situation. It's important to identify the context that the assumption developed in so you can assess whether there's congruence between the developmental environment and the current environment. Take a moment and reflect on the context of those early situations. For example, as a young child, did you feel powerless partially because you were a young child? That context is vital to understanding the assumption. Did someone important to you mistreat you in a major way? Are there factors about that person that makes them different from the average individual or the entirety of people?

In what context did the assumptions develop? And how does that context match the current situation?

Some important context is the fact that my dad has never really been impressed by anything. In fact, he's rather unemotional. It's not that he was proud of someone else and not proud of me. Rather, he's just emotionally distant.

In what context did the assumptions develop? And how does that context match the current situation?

_____

_____

_____

_____

_____

Is There a Vicious Cycle?

Vicious cycles exist where the response to the problem unwittingly perpetuates the problem. Examples of this might include someone quitting or avoiding difficult tasks for fear of failure. The unintended consequence of this behavior is a lack of success. You can't have successes if you're not willing to take risks. This creates a vicious cycle in that the person doesn't have successes to draw from when wondering about their abilities, and thus continues to buy into this fallacious self-narrative of being a failure. In truth, they're simply afraid of being a failure. So, the question to ask yourself is how you behave and respond in situations where this assumption is active. Often people respond with a control strategy or an avoid strategy, to try and minimize their discomfort. Typically, this path of least resistance, short-term coping drives long-term misery.

How do I respond when this assumption is activated? What are the long-term consequences of that behavior?

When I have a feeling that I'm not going to be good enough or a fear that I'm going to fail, I tend to overthink the situation and then avoid it entirely. This leaves me feeling exhausted and the long-term consequence is that I don't have a lot to show for my life. I'm essentially underemployed and under-achieved, which drives this self-narrative of being a failure.

How do I respond when this assumption is activated? What are the long-term consequences of that behavior?

_____

_____

_____

_____

_____

Are There Gaps in Knowledge and Experience?

People often have limited experiences based on their use of control strategies or avoid strategies. This lack of experiences results in a lack of corrective experiences. Sometimes from a scientific or philosophical perspective, active experimentation is needed to gather a representative sample of experiences. You have just looked at what you typically do when this assumption is active. Now you want to know which experiences and activities you haven't engaged in due to your assumptions. It might be that you need to identify activities to engage in to gather new experiences and new evidence, even for a period of time. Remember, if you're doing something new, it's highly likely that it won't be seamless the first time you do it. One of the challenging things about being a human is that we typically have to persist at being bad at something before we reach the point of being good at it. You might revisit this section at a later point after having developed new patterns of behavior.

What experiences and activities have I not engaged in due to my assumptions?

I typically don't try things I think I might fail at. I quit or avoid those activities for fear of failing. Consequently, I don't really know what my abilities would be if I were to really try. I gather I probably wouldn't be great at first and would need to persist in my efforts to develop the competency I want to have.

What experiences and activities have I not engaged in due to my assumptions?

_____

_____

_____

_____

_____

Are There Plausible Alternative Explanations?

This concept is explained well with the truism that *correlation isn't causation*. Sometimes two things might appear to be related but are not actually related. A common example of this includes the correlation between ice cream sales and homicide rates. Some data show that as more ice cream is sold, homicide rates increase. This correlations could lead someone to think that ice cream in itself is dangerous. However, a third variable accounts for the correlation: more ice cream tends to be sold in the summer and there are various factors associated with the summer, such as increased heat, that may better account for increases in homicide rates. Take a moment and ponder whether there are other potential variables that could be at play. Could some other factor or factors be influencing your results? Could certain situational contexts, behaviors, occurrences, or cultural factors play a role?

Are there other variables or factors to account for when considering my assumption?

Well, my assumption is largely influenced by my father. There could be factors about him that make it more a "him thing" and not a "me thing." For example, there might be reasons why he's under-emotional. I guess I never thought that it might be more about him than about me.

Are there other variables or factors to account for when considering my assumption?

_____

_____

_____

_____

_____

Filtering Out What Doesn't Match Assumptions

Often, our assumptions can be overgeneralizations of things that actually happened to us. To better understand the nuances of reality and our assumptions, it's important to note instances where your past assumptions were not true. Were there any exceptions to the rule? Were there times what you expected to happen didn't happen? It might be that some of these instances occurred without your noticing it. A frequent finding from social psychology is that people tend to see what they expect to see, and people tend to remember seeing what they expected to see.

The implications are that individuals often need to track and log the discrepant experiences they normally miss, simply because the mind often filters these out. It's important to spend time tracking or logging these things. For example, for someone who has beliefs about being incompetent, they likely fixate on their shortcomings and disregard their successes. This pattern of thinking augments their beliefs about competence. These people often benefit from keeping a running log of their accomplishments to help them have a more balanced recollection of what transpired.

Take a moment and consider what elements of an interaction you're most likely to attend to given your assumptions. For example, someone with an assumption that other people are rude and inconsiderate will likely miss instances where people are polite or courteous. Those with assumptions of incompetence will likely miss or filter out instances of competency or accomplishment. Individuals with assumptions that they'll be rejected or neglected are likely to filter out instances of neutrality or acceptance.

What am I most likely to miss in a situation?

I typically miss times when I do a good job or even an okay job. I get so worried about screwing up, or being found out to be a screwup, that I typically don't slow down and recognize my accomplishments.

What am I most likely to miss in a situation?

_____

_____

_____

Exceptions to Assumptions

Have you had any experiences that are exceptions to your assumption? You might need to spend some time tracking these exceptions to have a more balanced understanding of what happened. Sometimes a new behavioral pattern is needed in order to facilitate exceptions. For example, someone who has a fear of failing and tends to quit early at the first sign of failure won't have many successes to draw from. So, they might need to develop a new behavioral pattern in order to have new experiences that will be contrary to their assumptions.

What experiences stand out to me that are not consistent with my assumption?

Nothing major stands out. I tend to avoid major tasks for fear of failing. There have been a few times at work that I did a decent job and my supervisor told me I did a good job. I tend not to dwell on those though.

What experiences stand out to me that are not consistent with my assumption?

_____

_____

_____

_____

Functionality of the Assumption

A pragmatic approach is to consider the functionality of your assumption. This means to focus less on whether or not the assumption is empirically true, but rather on the outcome of the assumption. Is this a helpful assumption to have? How does believing this assumption affect your behavior, and in turn, what happens? Is there another way of looking at the situation that will motivate the type of behavior you're hoping to engage in?

What are the short- and long-term effects of believing my assumption?

By believing that I'm incompetent in the short term I have a lot of distress. I tend to engage in avoidance patterns, which undercut my long-term development and progression. The long-term effect of believing I'm incompetent is I'll appear as if I actually am incompetent because I haven't taken any real risks in my life.

What are the short- and long-term effects of believing my assumption?

_____

_____

_____

_____

_____

Other Evidence or Factors to Consider

Now examine whether there are any other pieces of evidence or factors that may affect the accuracy of your assumption. There may be other reasons to not believe your assumption.

Are there other facts or pieces of evidence that negate my assumption?

I guess when I was reading this workbook I came across the idea of double ignorance: not knowing what you're doing, and not knowing that you don't know what you're doing, is the most dangerous kind of ignorance. If I have shortcomings but I'm aware of those shortcomings, that's a competency in itself. It doesn't necessarily make me feel better, but it's nice to know I'm not naive to my shortcomings.

Are there other facts or pieces of evidence that negate my assumption?

_____

_____

_____

_____

_____

Step 4: Summary and Synthesis

The goal of this process is to take a step back, out from the depths of the assumption. From here, you're able to get a good look at what's going on and create a more balanced and accurate perspective. It's a challenge to mentally step out of the narrative you have and try to see things as they really are. Part of this process is recognizing that as a human, there are limits to your perceptual abilities. Knowing there may be things you don't know is the first step toward wisdom. In this final step, you'll develop a balanced summary of this entire dialogue.

Summary

The first stage in this process is to summarize the case against the assumption to create a more balanced view. Consider the following example, then do the exercise yourself. Take your time. Feel free to flip back between the pages you've written. This can be an emotionally laborious process, so take the time to consolidate the information.

What's an overall summary of my Socratic dialogue?

The assumption that I'm a failure is based on early interactions I had with my father. In these interactions, I always had the impression that nothing I ever did was good enough for him. The current support for my being a failure is my lack of successes or major achievements. Also, my procrastination and avoidance have resulted in job loss and job problems before. I recognize in this process some important contextual factors. For example, my father didn't appear to be proud of me, though he might just be an under-emotional guy and I need to not take that personally. I hadn't previously considered that it might be a "him problem," not necessarily a "me problem." Also, my lack of achievement seems to be driven by my fear of really trying. I'm more afraid of failing than quitting, and I've never really tested my true potential. I've had some successes at work; even though none of them are major, they still count. However, I do have the benefit of having some awareness of my shortcomings so that I'm not doubly ignorant.

What's an overall summary of my Socratic dialogue?

_____

_____

_____

_____

_____

_____

Synthesis

The first part of the elenctic method is to define the construct that will later be proved or disproved through the inquiry. At the start of this process, you developed a definition for the assumption to be evaluated. Further, you developed that definition into something more balanced and universal. In this step, you'll compare that universal definition with your summary statement. Here you will see whether the assumption has been proven to be true or whether there needs to be a modification to the assumption.

Restate my assumption.

My fear is that I'm a failure. Failure means quitting because I'm afraid instead of making a mistake. I can't be successful if I'm afraid of making mistakes.

Did the overall summary confirm my assumption?

No. I'm not a failure because I haven't yet quit, though I'm at risk for failing if I keep avoiding challenges. Paradoxically, my fear of failure might cause me to become a failure if I don't change.

Restate my assumption in a manner that's more consistent with the information learned from the Socratic dialogue.

I'm only a failure if I live a life of fear and avoidance. Facing my fears and challenging myself actually puts me on the path toward success.

Restate my assumption.

_____

_____

Did the overall summary confirm my assumption?

_____

_____

Restate my assumption in a manner that's more consistent with the information learned from the Socratic dialogue.

_____

_____

This dialogue is one conversation in a lifetime of development. As you identify the behaviors that corresponded to your old assumptions, also reflect on the behaviors that will contribute to a cultivation of your new assumption. What behaviors are in keeping with your values and Stoic virtues? To put it simply, insight is good, but insight plus behavior change is better.

Chapter 10 Takeaways

- You can learn to think like Socrates to overcome your self-limiting beliefs.

- The first step is identifying a belief to focus on.

- Next, build an understanding of how the belief developed.

- Then use curiosity to expand your perspective to see what you're missing.

- Finally, use summary and synthesis strategies to create a new balanced perspective and course of action.

References

Adams-Clark, A. A., X. Yang, M. N. Lind, C. G. Martin, and M. Zalewski. 2022. "I'm Sorry: A New DBT Skill for Effective Apology." *DBT Bulletin* 6(1): 29–30.

Addison, J. 1713. *Cato: A Tragedy. As It Is Acted at the Theatre-Royal in Drury-Lane, by Her Majesty's Servants.* London: Shakespear's Head.

Aurelius, M. 2003. *Meditations: Living, Dying and the Good Life.* Translated by G. Hays. London: Phoenix.

———. 2013. *Meditations, Books 1–6.* Translated by C. Gill. London: Oxford University Press.

Beck, A. T. 1976. *Cognitive Therapy and the Emotional Disorders.* New York: Meridian.

———. 1989. *Love Is Never Enough: How Couples Can Overcome Misunderstandings, Resolve Conflicts, and Solve Relationship Problems through Cognitive Therapy.* New York: Harper & Row.

Beck, A. T., and E. A. P. Haigh. 2014. "Advances in Cognitive Theory and Therapy: The Generic Cognitive Model." *Annual Review of Clinical Psychology* 10: 1–24.

Brach, T. 2004. *Radical Acceptance: Embracing Your Life with the Heart of a Buddha.* New York: Bantam.

Chiaradonna, R., and R. C. G. Galluzzo. 2013. *Universals in Ancient Philosophy.* Pisa: Edizioni Della Normale.

Dillon, J., ed. 2003. *The Greek Sophists.* London: Penguin.

Dodds, E. R. 1990. *Gorgias: A Revised Text, with Introduction and Commentary.* New York: Clarendon Press.

Ellis, A. 1962. *Reason and Emotion in Psychotherapy: A Comprehensive Method of Treating Human Disturbance.* Secaucus, NJ: Citadel.

————. 2005. *The Myth of Self-Esteem: How Rational Emotive Behavior Therapy Can Change Your Life Forever.* Buffalo, NY: Prometheus Books.

Epictetus. 1995. *The Discourses: The Handbook, Fragments.* Translated by R. Hard. Edited by C. Gill and R. Stoneman. London: Everyman.

Gilbert, P. 2009. "Introducing Compassion-Focused Therapy." *Advances in Psychiatric Treatment* 15(3): 199–208.

Gilbert, P., and S. Procter. 2006. "Compassionate Mind Training for People with High Shame and Self-Criticism: Overview and Pilot Study of a Group Therapy Approach." *Clinical Psychology & Psychotherapy* 13(6): 353–379.

Gill, C. 2010. *Naturalistic Psychology in Galen and Stoicism.* London: Oxford University Press.

Graver, M. R. 2019. *Stoicism and Emotion.* Chicago: University of Chicago Press.

Greenberg, L. S. 2004. "Emotion-Focused Therapy." *Clinical Psychology & Psychotherapy* 11(1): 3–16.

Grimes, P., and R. L. Uliana. 1998. *Philosophical Midwifery: A New Paradigm for Understanding Human Problems with Its Validation.* Costa Mesa, CA: Hyparxis Press.

Harper, K. 2014. *Cato, Roman Stoicism, and the American "Revolution."* Sydney: University of Sydney.

Hayes, S. C., K. D. Strosahl, and K. G. Wilson. 2016. *Acceptance and Commitment Therapy: The Process and Practice of Mindful Change.* New York: Guilford Press.

Holiday, R. 2014. *The Obstacle Is the Way: Turning Adversity into Advantage.* New York: Portfolio.

————. 2016. *Ego Is the Enemy.* New York: Portfolio.

Holiday, R., and S. Hanselman. 2020. *Lives of the Stoics: The Art of Living from Zeno to Marcus Aurelius.* London: Penguin.

King, C. 2011. *Musonius Rufus: Lectures and Sayings.* Seattle: CreateSpace.

LeBon, T. 2022. *365 Ways to Be More Stoic: A Day-by-Day Guide to Practical Stoicism.* London: John Murray One.

Linehan, M. M. 2014. *DBT Skills Training Manual,* 2nd ed. New York: Guilford Press.

Maslow, A. H. 1966. *The Psychology of Science: A Reconnaissance*. New York: Harper & Row.

Nehamas, A. 1998. *The Art of Living: Socratic Reflections from Plato to Foucault*, vol. 61. Berkeley, CA: University of California Press.

Overholser, J. C. 2018. *The Socratic Method of Psychotherapy*. New York: Columbia University Press.

Padesky, C. A. 1993. "Socratic Questioning: Changing Minds or Guiding Discovery." Paper presented at the European Congress of Behavioural and Cognitive Therapies, London. http://padesky.com/newpad/wpcontent/uploads/2012/11/socquest.pdf.

Pangle, T. L. 2018. *The Socratic Way of Life: Xenophon's "Memorabilia."* Chicago: University of Chicago Press.

Peterson, C., and M. E. P. Seligman. 2004. *Character Strengths and Virtues: A Handbook and Classification*. New York: Oxford University Press.

Pigliucci, M., and G. Lopez. 2019. *A Handbook for New Stoics: How to Thrive in a World Out of Your Control—52 Week-by-Week Lessons*. New York: The Experiment.

Plato. 1997. *Complete Works*. Edited by J. M. Cooper and D. S. Hutchinson. Indianapolis, IN: Hackett.

Plutarch. 1914. *Lives*. Translated by B. Perrin. Cambridge, MA: Harvard University Press.

Polat, B. B. 2019. *Tranquility Parenting: A Guide to Staying Calm, Mindful, and Engaged*. Lanham, MD: Rowman & Littlefield.

Ramelli, I. 2009. *Hierocles the Stoic*. Cardiff, UK: Sanderson Books.

Robertson, D. 2010. *The Philosophy of Cognitive-Behavioral Therapy: Stoicism as Rational and Cognitive Psychotherapy*. London: Karnac.

——. 2012. *Build Your Resilience: CBT, Mindfulness and Stress Management to Survive and Thrive in Any Situation*. London: Teach Yourself.

——. 2013. *Stoicism and the Art of Happiness*. London: Teach Yourself.

——. 2019. *How to Think Like a Roman Emperor: The Stoic Philosophy of Marcus Aurelius*. New York: St. Martin's Press.

Robb, H. 2022. *Willingly ACT for Spiritual Development: Acknowledge, Choose, & Teach Others*. Long Beach, NY: Valued Living Books.

Sellars, J. 2013. *The Art of Living: The Stoics on the Nature and Function of Philosophy*, 2nd ed. London: Bloomsbury Academic.

———. 2020. *The Pocket Stoic*. Chicago: University of Chicago Press.

Seneca. 1917–1925. *Moral Epistles*, vol. 1. Translated by R. M. Gummere. Cambridge, MA: Harvard University Press.

———. 2004. *Letters from a Stoic*. Translated by R. Campbell. Harmondsworth, UK: Penguin.

Stankiewicz, P. 2020. *Manual of Reformed Stoicism*. Wilmington, DE: Vernon Press.

Tee, J., and N. Kazantzis. 2011. "Collaborative Empiricism in Cognitive Therapy: A Definition and Theory for the Relationship Construct." *Clinical Psychology: Science and Practice* 18(1): 47–61.

Tirch, D., L. R. Silberstein-Tirch, R. T. Codd III, M. J. Brock, and M. J. Wright. 2019. *Experiencing ACT from the Inside Out: A Self-Practice/Self-Reflection Workbook for Therapists*. New York: Guilford Press.

Vlastos, G. 1991. *Socrates, Ironist and Moral Philosopher*, vol. 50. Ithaca, NY: Cornell University Press.

Waltman, S. H., R. T. Codd, L. M. McFarr, and B. A. Moore. 2020. *Socratic Questioning for Therapists and Counselors: Learn How to Think and Intervene Like a Cognitive Behavior Therapist*. New York: Routledge.

Waltman, S. H., and A. Palermo. 2019. "Theoretical Overlap and Distinction between Rational Emotive Behavior Therapy's Awfulizing and Cognitive Therapy's Catastrophizing." *Mental Health Review Journal* 24(1): 44–50.

Waltman, S., and L. Sokol. 2017. "The Generic Cognitive Model of Cognitive Behavioral Therapy: A Case Conceptualization-Driven Approach." In *The Science of Cognitive Behavioral Therapy*, edited by S. Hofmann and G. Asmundson. London: Academic Press.

Xenophon. 1970. *Memoirs of Socrates and the Symposium*. Translated by H. Treddenick. Harmondsworth, UK: Penguin.

Scott Waltman, PsyD, is a practicing Stoic, and international cognitive behavioral therapy (CBT) trainer. He was a Global Ambassador for the World Confederation of Cognitive and Behavioural Therapies. He is a board member of the International Association of Cognitive Behavioral Therapy, and president-elect of the Academy of Cognitive and Behavioral Therapies (A-CBT). He is coauthor of *Socratic Questioning for Therapists and Counselors*. He lives in San Antonio, TX.

R. Trent Codd III, EdS, is vice president of clinical services in the Carolinas for Refresh Mental Health. Prior to assuming his current position, he was executive director of the Cognitive Behavioral Therapy Center of Western North Carolina, a multidisciplinary group practice specializing in the provision of evidence-based mental health care, a practice he founded in 2001. In addition, he is a diplomate, fellow, and certified trainer/consultant for the A-CBT, and a board-certified behavior analyst (BCBA). Codd has authored and coauthored several peer-reviewed publications and books, including *Socratic Questioning for Therapists and Counselors*. He lives in Asheville, NC.

Kasey Pierce is a writer, editor, and Stoic columnist from the Metro Detroit, MI, area. She was a freelance content editor on Donald Robertson's *Verissimus*, editor of Tim LeBon's *365 Ways to Be More Stoic*, and a recurring speaker at Stoicon-X Women. A graduate of business leadership studies, she was a speaker at Plato's Academy Centre's Ancient Philosophy for Modern Leadership conference. Pierce is passionate about broadening Stoicism's appeal, and feels CBT practices are the most efficient way of applying the ancient philosophy to everyday life.

Foreword writer **Donald J. Robertson** is author of six books, including *How to Think Like a Roman Emperor* and the graphic novel *Verissimus*, about the life and philosophy of Marcus Aurelius. He is a cognitive-behavioral psychotherapist, writer, and trainer who specializes in the relationship between philosophy, psychology, and self-improvement.

Real change *is* possible

For more than forty-five years, New Harbinger has published proven-effective self-help books and pioneering workbooks to help readers of all ages and backgrounds improve mental health and well-being, and achieve lasting personal growth. In addition, our spirituality books offer profound guidance for deepening awareness and cultivating healing, self-discovery, and fulfillment.

Founded by psychologist Matthew McKay and Patrick Fanning, New Harbinger is proud to be an independent, employee-owned company. Our books reflect our core values of integrity, innovation, commitment, sustainability, compassion, and trust. Written by leaders in the field and recommended by therapists worldwide, New Harbinger books are practical, accessible, and provide real tools for real change.

MORE BOOKS from
NEW HARBINGER PUBLICATIONS

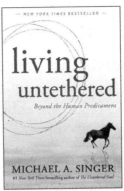

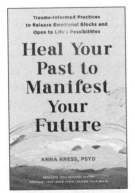
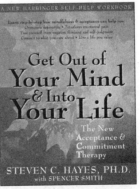

Did you know there are **free tools** you can download for this book?

Free tools are things like **worksheets**, **guided meditation exercises**, and **more** that will help you get the most out of your book.

You can download free tools for this book—whether you bought or borrowed it, in any format, from any source—from the New Harbinger website. All you need is a NewHarbinger.com account. Just use the URL provided in this book to view the free tools that are available for it. Then, click on the "download" button for the free tool you want, and follow the prompts that appear to log in to your NewHarbinger.com account and download the material.

You can also save the free tools for this book to your **Free Tools Library** so you can access them again anytime, just by logging in to your account! Just look for this button on the book's free tools page.

+ Save this to my free tools library

If you need help accessing or downloading free tools, visit **newharbinger.com/faq** or contact us at **customerservice@newharbinger.com**.